IS THIS WHAT THEY DIED FOR?

DR. D. K. OLUKOYA

IS THIS WHAT THEY DIED FOR?
© 2005 DR. D. K. OLUKOYA
ISBN-978-37254-9-1
1st Printing – April 2005 AD

Published by:

The Battle Cry Christian Ministries

322, Herbert Macaulay Street, Sabo, Yaba, P. O. Box 12272,
Ikeja, Lagos.

Phone: 0803-304-4239,01-8044415

All Scripture quotations are from the King James Version of the Bible

Cover illustration: Sister Shade Olukoya

TABLE OF CONTENTS

IS THIS WHAT THEY DIED FOR? 4

IF YOU WANT TO BE IN GOD'S INNER CIRCLE 19

THE SON OF PERDITION 37

THE SHRINE OF SELF 56

WANTED; MEMBERS OF DANIEL BAND 80

CHAPTER ONE
IS THIS WHAT THEY DIED FOR?

W e come across some life changing words in the third verse of the book of Jude.

Beloved, when I gave all diligence to write unto you of the common salvation, it was needful for me to write unto you, and exhort you that ye should earnestly contend for the faith which was once delivered unto the saints (Jude 3).

This passage refers to the precious faith, which was once delivered to the saints of old. To understand the importance of the above passage you will have to read another passage of the Bible. This passage highlights a group of men whose lives have remained a challenge to generations.

Women receive their dead raised to life again: and others were tortured, not accepting deliverance; that they might obtain a better resurrection: And others had trial of cruel mocking and scourging, yea, moreover of bonds and imprisonment: They were stoned, they were sawn asunder, were tempted, were slain with the sword: they wandered about in sheepskins and goatskins being destitute, afflicted, tormented; (Of whom the world was not worthy): they wandered in deserts, and in mountains and in dens and caves of he earth. And these all, having obtained a good report through faith, received not the promise: God having provided some better thing for us, that they without us should not be made perfect (Hebrews 11:35-40).

There are lots of challenges to draw concerning the life of the pioneers of our faith. They are worthy examples. Their lives stand out as monumental examples today.

To wrap these two passages, the Bible gives us another challenge in 1 Corinthians 10:12-13.

Wherefore let him that thinketh he standeth take heed lest he fall. There hath no temptation taken you but such as is common to man: but God is faithful, who will not suffer you to be tempted above that ye are able; but will with the temptation also make a way to escape, that ye may be able to bear it.

We are instructed to take heed lest we fall. What does the Bible mean by the phrase – "take heed." It simply means that we must be watchful and cautious. It also means, we should be vigilant and observant. It also means that we must take heed of the path which we are treading. It is extremely dangerous for you to take unwarranted risk over your Christian life. No matter how sure you are, you must never take anything for granted.

Some people go about manifesting false confidence, they believe that nothing will ever happen to them. Even if you are a Sunday School teacher or pastor, you must still take heed. Somebody may feel that he is standing, whereas he is already fallen flat on the floor. When the Bible says take heed, everybody is included.

One of the saddest days in my life was when I came across a man who was just coming out of a popular blue-light district in Lagos, Nigeria. From the way he was adjusting his trousers, it was obvious that he had gone to visit a prostitute. To my surprise, he was singing: "It is well with my soul." From the way he was singing, it became clear to me that he must be a backslider. I couldn't believe my ears as I heard him sing all the stanzas of the hymn.

The curiosity in me made me to double my steps in order to catch up with him, "Mr.", I said, "Are you a Christian? The way you sang that song made me feel that you must have been a born-again Christian. Did anything go wrong along the line?"

He listened to me patiently and said: "To be honest with you brother, some things actually went wrong with me. I can't deny what I have done, but it is not my fault. My pastor did such a terrible mistake that I decided to visit a prostitute out of a kind of holy anger. Why should my pastor do what he did? I just felt that, if a pastor could do that, then I can go ahead to commit immorality with a prostitute."

I shook my head when I discovered that the man once had the touch of heaven upon his life. He seemed not to realise the gravity of what he had done as he kept on saying: "As long as that man remains the pastor of our church, I am going to backslide further."

I tried to help him further. "Listen to me," I said, "Don't make anyone your standard. You are only accountable to God. The Bible says each of us shall give account of himself unto God at the judgement seat of Christ, to receive a reward for what we have done, whether it is good or bad. You are going to face the judgement seat as an individual, your pastor will not accompany you to the judgement seat of Christ. If you are a Christian and decide to backslide, you are responsible for your action."

Nothing should be powerful enough to make a believer backslide. Hunger, persecution, nakedness and other problems of life should not take you from the love of Christ.

It is unfortunate that many so-called believers have looked back like Lot's wife. When a vehicle turns to the left or right, it has the tendency of going back to where it is coming from. Heaven-bound pilgrims do not look back. If you look back, you may lose your salvation.

What have you got to do alone in a room with a woman, who happens not to be your wife? I pity so-called believers who are so confident that they feel that they cannot fall. Such people have forgotten that a servant of God like Paul, the apostle said: "For we have no confidence in the flesh."

Those who need to be extra-careful in the area of immorality are not only single people; the married are inclusive. Marriage is not a security that you cannot fall into the sin of fornication. If you place your salvation under a risk, you may fall. Don't ever deceive yourself saying that you can dine with the devil by using the proverbial "long spoon."

This reminds me of the story of a particular man who came for prayer and counselling, some ten years ago. Unfortunately, the man started his journey into the land of immorality with masturbation. Many so-called Christians are involved in that deadly sin. The devil deceived him further until he was hooked to a loaf of bread as his wife. By the time he came for prayer and deliverance, he had gone deeper into sin. In fact, he was doing abominable things. Things got so bad that he started sleeping with ducks. He never bargained for such deadly bondage. When he started with masturbation, he was so sure that he could stop whenever he wanted. At the end of the day, he was deeply enmeshed in a bondage which he found difficult to gain freedom from.

Perhaps, the Spirit of the Lord warned you against certain sins. Maybe, you turned deaf ears believing that you are wise or mature enough to handle the devil. Of course, you knew what you were trying to do was bad, but you gave yourself a false hope, claiming that if you ever get into it, you will get out.

Many Christians hold certain erroneous views. They

believe that they are so strong spiritually that they can never fall. They go about telling everyone that those who are falling are only weak spiritually. They believe that anyone who falls is only stupid.

Some people are so confident that they say, "At my age? Why should I ever have any problem with immorality at age fifty? Do not ever have any form of confidence in the flesh.

Unfortunately, financial prosperity has introduced false security into the lives of people. Wealth has cast people into the state of ease and lured them to sleep. The Bible says. "Woe unto those that are in ease in Zion."

Beloved, if you are not careful, you can begin to get familiar with sin, in small degrees. When the sin that used to sadden you when you got newly converted, no longer alarms you, something is terribly wrong with you. Whenever the sins that use to make you shiver and catch cold begins to look insignificant to you, something is wrong somewhere. "Let him that thinketh he standeth take heed, lest he fall."

Some Christian sisters have allowed the devil to deceive them to start the journey into the land of worldliness by accommodating tiny earrings. They have taken further a journey by graduating into using bigger earrings. If care is not taken, they may go back into the world totally. They may go from using jewellery into using wigs and attachment and putting on trousers. From that situation, spiritual husbands will step into their lives.

When such a problem comes up, they run to the deliverance ground where they get temporary relief. As soon as they experience relief, they go back into the same sin and the devil catches up with them again.

Many modern day Christians are proud and over-confident. A lot of people do not know that the devil presents temptation in an attractive form. He dangles the bait while he conceals the hook. The devil is so subtle that he might catch you before you ever realise what is happening.

I almost shed tears, some years ago, when I came across a man of God who had fallen flat on his face. He came with eyes filled with tears seeking help and deliverance. Although he was married with children, the devil caught him by using a woman as a bait. As soon as the woman knew that the adulterous act had been concluded, she came up with an outburst of a sinister laughter, "Now we have caught you; we've been trying to catch you for the past seventeen years."

After that experience, his ministry nose- dived. Many say like a foolish old man, "Give me a glass and I will not become a drunkard." But before he knew what was happening, he had already become drunk.

I want you to learn a lesson from the life of Reuben, one of the sons of Jacob. If you have read his dossier among the children of Jacob, you will conclude that he must have been a scientist. Jacob had a brilliant understanding of the lives of each of his children.

Concerning Reuben, he said: "Reuben, you are as unstable as water." Water is so consistently inconsistent that it will always follow the path of least resistance. Whenever water comes in contact with a cold atmosphere, it freezes. When it comes in contact with heat, it boils. Water can fit into any container, be it small or big.

Unfortunately, Reuben's unstable character got transferred unto his descendants. According to the book of Judges, when Deborah and Barak asked everyone to come out and fight, the tribe of Reuben was no where in sight. They were busy listening to the music of the shepherd. They preferred the flute of the shepherd to following the trumpet of war. Unfortunately, we have a large population of the children of Reuben in our churches today. They troop out of the church even before the service is over. Such people are not committed to God at all.

Many pioneers of the Christian faith actually sealed their faith with their blood. They died for the cause of the gospel and shed their blood for the master.

Let me ask you a crucial question. I have actually spent nights crying myself out while searching for an answer to the question.

Are we really practising what these people died for? Are we really contending for the faith today? I have discovered that many are contending for their pockets and their bellies. Such people do not know that as long as they continue to fight for their pockets, prosperity will be far away from them. They have forgotten that it is more blessed to give than to receive.

As the General Overseer of Mountain of Fire and Miracles Ministries, I have made up my mind that I will continue to contend for the faith. Money does not mean anything to me. For example God brings millions of naira in to the ministry through our recorded audio ministry. Do you know that whatever comes out of the sale of the cassettes is plowed back into the ministry? We have never taken out a dime of the proceeds into our private pockets. Everything goes into the ministry. If we have decided to amass wealth, may be God would not have been blessing us the way He had been doing.

If we undertake a survey of what many of us are doing, can we truly say that our present standard of Christianity is worth the matter that the martyrs of the faith died for? Some of the martyrs of the Christian faith were cut in two, others slain with the sword. We share in the same faith with these martyrs. Some people sing: "I am going higher, yes I am", without knowing what they are saying. Whereas, the first man who sang the song was thrown into the bottom of the sea from where he sang: "I'm going higher, yes I am." He was not singing the song while lying on a bed of roses.

The Christians of those days were stripped of their possessions, driven out of their homes, robbed of their prospects. In those days, believers were put to the test with the question: "Do you belief in the Lord Jesus?" If they ever said yes; they cut off their fingers with giant scissors. By the time the pain subsides, the same question will be asked. Another positive answer will lead to another chopping off of another finger. There were occasions in church history where people's ears were chopped off. The victims of such cruel torture were made to run miles to make them bleed to death.

Christians were driven away from their homes. Whenever there was an earthquake, Christians were accused, rounded off and slaughtered like bulls. These men sealed their testimony with their blood, young or old. They were dealt with, with utmost cruelty. They were set on fire until they were burnt to death. Whenever the victims ran around, the fire burning them would provide light for the persecutors to see in darkness. Many of them were burnt alive. Many of them were thrown into ancient amphitheatres where many watched them being fed to lions.

My heart was touched the other day when I read about the story of one sister call Perpetual. Each reading brought tears into my eyes. She happened to be a faithful 22-year-old who was sold out for Jesus. She was arrested because of her commitment to the Lord.

"Are you ready to offer sacrifice to this our idol?" She was asked.

"No!" she said, "I am a Christian!"

They were angry with her. Her father pleaded passionately with her; "Don't kill yourself prematurely. Why must you die because of Christianity? You are such an intelligent girl. "

The father kept crying behind her as she was dragged to where she would be killed. To make her budge, sister Perpetual's father was bundled and thrown into the bush like rubbish. At that time, sister Perpetual had just given birth to a baby. In fact, she was still breast-feeding. Both she and her new baby were taken into prison. Later her father was brought to her where she was in prison.

The persecutors forced Perpetual's father to forcefully pluck up his beards and the hair on his head and place the bloody hair on the floor. While he did this, he continued to plead with her daughter. That was enough to move even the most decided person to change his mind.

Perpetual went through all kinds of torture. The lady was later brought into an amphitheatre and a wild bull was let-loose on her. The bull smashed itself against her and broke her bones. The persecutors were very wicked. They brought sister Perpetual to the theatre fresh from child birth and stripped her naked. Fresh milk was dropping from her breasts. After the bull had brought her down to the floor. Some soldiers came towards her with a sword in their hands. She did not even wait for the soldiers to cut her into pieces. She held a soldier's hand and applied the knife to her own throat.

If these martyrs died in such a manner, can our present Christians be described as living out what they died for? Other martyrs were thrown into an arena where they were torn into pieces by mad dogs. People actually paid to watch Christians die. Multitudes gathered applauding and clapping because of the painful way the Christians were dying. The agony of dying martyrs provided entertainment to the unbelievers.

Christians were hunted like animals of prey. They were forced to hide in desperate and solitary places. Their earthly possessions did not make them renounce Christ. Many of these martyrs suffered untold agony.

Today, when modern day believers are offended in small matters, they say: "It is enough, I will never step into their church again." When they do what is wrong and they are placed under suspension; they run to another church. Once some so-called Christian sisters experience some delay in getting husbands, they begin to put on bangles and earrings and go the way of the world.

Be assured of this, a godly man cannot go for an ungodly, worldly lady. Therefore, a lady who wants to marry a godly husband should be godly. Many Christian sisters have either tainted or coloured their hair. Those who style their hair, like the people of the world, do not know where they are going yet. If the martyrs of the early Christian era were to look at what you are doing presently, would they admit that this is what they died for?

A man was arraigned before his executioners with his four children and his wife. He was asked: "Are you insisting that you want to stick to Jesus?" "Yes!" the man shouted. The persecutors were infuriated, they dragged out his eldest son and beheaded him, the head rolled towards the man's leg. They asked the man for the second time; "Do you still want to stick to your Jesus?" They angrily cut off the head of the second boy. When they discovered that the brother was not moved by their wicked actions, they dragged out his wife as if they were about to cut off her own neck. At that moment, the man was moved to tears. His faith began to waver, at that moment, the younger daughter shouted: "Daddy, don't deny Christ." Out of anger, the persecutor cut the little girl into pieces.

If the Christians of those days could suffer all these, what are we doing today? Is this what they died for? Are we going to the same heaven with these martyrs? If we are going to the same heaven with those who sealed their faith with their blood, how come many of us have time for gossiping and backbiting?

Are you considering your heavenly crown in view of the present scheme of things?

Some Christians were gathered and buried alive. The persecutors were so wicked that they left one leg of each buried believer outside. Some of them were also buried with parts of their bodies above ground level. These believers died painfully.

What kind of Christianity are we practising today?

I once met a white man who had a fearful dream, he was not a serious Christian before, but that dream jolted him out of complacency into vibrant faith. He had a revelation in which he found himself in heaven. He came across a fellow who told him: "I have been in heaven here for the past 1860 years. Do you know how I got here? The persecutors covered me with flammable materials and I was set ablaze. I was burnt for Jesus." The brother said: "That must have been a very horrible death." "Now I am happy, I have entered the joy of my Father. My Father told me: 'Well done, good and faithful servant.'"

He met another fellow who told him: "Do you know how I got here? I came in here, exactly 500 years ago. We went to preach in a particular village. The villagers surrounded where we were sleeping, killed me and cooked me in a pot." The two believers whom he met in heaven told him: "This is what we suffered for the master, what have you suffered for him?" By the time the brother woke up the next day, he was sweating profusely.

You claim to be going to heaven, yet you loose your temper. You put attachment to your hair. It is that attachment that will first get burnt in hell fire, if you die as a backslider. You better discard all the worldly dresses which you have been putting on and dress like a child of God.

Matthias replaced Judas. Do you know how he died? He was stoned and beheaded at last.

Andrew was also crucified on the cross. The two ends of the cross were fixed to the ground.

For Mark, idol worshippers dragged him on the floor until his body peeled and was cut to pieces.

Peter knew that he was going to die. He had an opportunity to escape and he did. On his way out he saw Jesus coming. He asked Jesus, "Where are you going?" Jesus said, "I am going in to be crucified the second time because of you." As soon as Peter heard that, he quickly went back and surrendered himself to be crucified.

How did Paul, the apostle die? They cut off his head.

Jude was also crucified.

Bartholomew was cruelly beaten and crucified.

Thomas, the one that is popularly known as the doubter was killed with a spear.

Luke, the writer of the gospel was hanged on a tree.

John, the beloved was the only apostle who escaped violent death. Attempts were made to kill him, it was just that he did not die. He was thrown into boiling oil but did not die.

Phillip was also crucified.

Matthew, the gospel writer was slain with the sword.

The question I would like to ask you at this point is, is this what these Christian martyrs died for?

Where do you stand today? Are you weighed and found wanting? Why don't you ask God to search and examine your heart today? Why don't you ask Him to prepare you for heaven?

I wish you could see the Lord's face, you'll be shocked to discover how angry He is.

CHAPTER 2

IF YOU WANT TO BE IN GOD'S INNER CIRCLE . . .

Faith in God is the beginning of experiencing the supernatural. As it is among men, relationship with God has different levels. There are casual friends and there are bosom friends. There are distant relations and there are immediate ones. Everyone in the world can describe the levels of relationships he has with others.

There is the general class of believers in God's family. They are contented with just conversion experience. These believers listen to the same message stuff. God deals with them at the same level of relationship. The experiences of the children of God in this group are common and similar. Their characteristics easily distinguish them from others in different groups.

There is another group of believers who belong to the middle class. They can be described as having gone a step away from the first category. God relates with them at a level higher than that of the first class. The messages they receive from God are higher in substance and standard. While the first class of believers are satisfied with just the milk of God's word, the middle class go beyond that to seek the flesh they can chew.

The last category of believers is the third class. This class is not made up of the majority. One of the distinguishing factors of these believers is their scarcity in every generation. You don't find many in this class in a single generation. In the history of God's moves, they are found scantily here and there in dispensational distribution.

This third class of believers is otherwise known as the inner circle of God. God reveals His deep secrets to them. Others in the first and second categories are not privileged to know the secrets made available to those in the inner circle. The believers here are God's confidants. They despise milk and ignore flesh, they run after the strong bones of God's revelations.

The choice of where you belong is yours. In this chapter, you are going to discover that the heartbeat of

God and His urgent call point to the fact that men and women are urgently needed in the inner circle. You will discover what to do to belong to God's inner circle. Don't be deceived, God has favourites. The decision to be a favourite is yours. If however you want to belong to other groups, the choice is yours. God has favourites.

You can decide to be as close to God as you want. God is always available at any level of relationship. He does not drive those that choose to come to Him. If you are willing to be close to Him, God will open the door for you. The choice is simply yours. It is written in the word of God: "Draw near to God and He will draw near to you." If you choose to stand aloof, God will keep aloof from you. Your degree of closeness to God depends on your desire. Read the text below.

Amos 3:7: Surely the Lord GOD will do nothing, but he revealeth his secret unto his servants the prophets.

It is a wonderful thing to be in the inner circle of God. There are some people who know the programmes of God. There are people who can foretell what will happen in a country in the next seven years. Sometimes, what such people know are not permitted to be shared with everybody. The reason is that God restricts some knowledge only to those in the inner circle. He limits some revelations only to His favourites. Imagine what Amos said in the above text. Imagine that God cannot hide His secrets from some people. How wonderful it is to be one of such!

Elijah was an executive man of God. He communed

with God as though seeing Him face to face. It was like belonging to the executive meeting of God. His knowledge of God and revelations portray him as a man who was part of God's council of decision making.

Micaiah was another man in the Bible of similar experience and privilege like Elijah. His story in the Bible does not span many chapters and verses. He was not described with elaborate genealogy and diary of signs and wonders. The picture that readily comes to mind of a man like him is of a lone-ranger in the ministry of the prophets. Four hundred prophets of Ahab, the king of Israel, stood and prophesied in unison. They all foresaw peace, safety and victory in the battle ahead of the king at Ramoth-Gilead. But Micaiah was a divergent voice. He saw what others did not see because he belonged to God's inner circle.

You see, people in the inner circle of God do not talk the way others do generally. Their messages are radically different from others. Their positions are considered strange and extreme in defence of God's course.

The king of Israel was reluctant to approach Micaiah to inquire of the Lord from him. Micaiah was not a prophet whose prophesies were suitable and comfortable to rulers and kings that did evil in the sight of the Lord. His prophecy therefore radically departed from the direction of other prophecies, because there was something in the invisible realm behind his position.

A conference was held in heaven. A committee of the God head sat. Micaiah was invited as a special guest. The Almighty summoned the hosts of heaven and all the spirits in the invisible realm gathered before Him. Micaiah spoke in a way not common in the Bible in recounting this awesome experience. He said: "I saw God sitting on a throne and the hosts of heaven stood before Him." That was frightening and very strange.

Micaiah continued with the details of the meeting held in heaven. He said as the committee sat, the topic on the agenda was Ahab. The decision to be taken was not in favour of the ignorant king and his deluded prophets. Micaiah was a prophet with a special privilege. The way he related his message to Ahab showed that he had attended the meeting called in heaven by God. He spoke with the authority and accuracy of a secretary that took the minutes of the meeting.

That man was allowed to see what was going on in the highest council in heaven. What a glorious experience it is to walk in that realm! When you enter into this realm, unbelief flies away and people misconstrue your confession of faith for bragging. In that realm, you will move closer to God because you belong to God's inner circle.

Moses prayed for seventy elders of Israel and God put His Spirit upon them. They began to prophesy because of the spirit of prophecy that rested on them. Of the seventy divinely elected to have a share of the spirit, two were not where others gathered. But because their hearts were attuned to that expectation, the overflow of the anointing caught them.

Men look at the face, but God looks at the hearts. These two began to prophesy like their counterparts who stood before Moses. Some zealous people reacted, expecting Moses to stop them but, Moses knew better. He said "I would God make everyone of His people prophets."

In the Mountain of Fire and Miracles Ministries, you can hear God. You are not prevented from hearing the Almighty. The work will be easier done if everybody is hearing God. My sisters, you can hear God. My brothers, you can hear God. When this happens, there will be no problem, at all. Every time we gather, we just celebrate Jesus.

This message is for those that want to be in the inner circle. They want to win before they fight. They want to see the outcome of the battle before they fight the battle. They are those who will stand confidently and say, 'The Lord whom I serve had told me this would happen before it happened'. Whatever people say will not matter to them. They are the people that will not celebrate the words of lawyers, they are people that will not take the words of doctors as final. They celebrate the authority of the word of God.

Unfortunately for this generation, it is full of people looking at the hands of God and not His face. They look to what they can get and receive from Him, not the expression on His face. It may sound strange to you that you can decide to look away from the hands of God to His face and ask Him, "What do you want me to do for you?" Those that distinguish themselves with God are not looking for what God can do for them, but what they can do for God.

One day, look God in the face and say to Him: "Do you have any problem you want me to solve for you?" You will get the shock of your life to hear him say: "Yes I have."

One of the major problems of God is expressed in Matthew. Read the text below.

Matthew 9:37- 38: Then saith he unto his disciples, The harvest truly [is] plenteous, but the labourers [are] few; Pray ye therefore the Lord of the harvest, that he will send forth labourers into his harvest.

There is plenteous harvest and there are few labourers. The programme of God is going through scarcity of labour. This is a serious concern in the heart of God. God is looking for Generals. There is no discrimination in His search. He is looking for men Generals and women Generals. He is looking for men and women who will lead this generation for Jesus. There are always vacancies for God's Generals in heaven.

The inner circle of God still have vacancies. There are five hundred disciples that followed Jesus at a time. That was a class for everybody. But the number soon got smaller. After the seventy disciples, twelve again were chosen. Among the twelve that were chosen, three were yet selected: Peter, James and John. Even among these three, John, the beloved was so chosen that Jesus' love for him could not be doubted. You can be as close to God as you personally want to be.

This question is a very serious one. When you live this world, what will be written down about you? At your burial, what comments would people pass? Would they be happy you were born or just conclude you with general cases of the dead? Would the people be able to trace your steps on the sand of time?

Many people are tired of being pushed here and there. But the problem is that our spiritual hands are too short to battle with some powers. God is looking for Generals. He is searching for them day and night. The Bible says the eyes of the Lord are going to and fro from the earth looking for men whose hearts are right with Him. Immediately He finds such people, He enlists them in His army.

Paul was a General in the army of God. He was beheaded. Peter was another General. He was crucified upside down. Martin Luther was another General. Smith Wigglesworth was another General in the army of God. He earned the title: Apostle of faith. The great Apostle Ayo Babalola was another General. He led his team of warriors on terrible onslaughts against satanic cohorts and came out victoriously.

These were some of the men who entered forbidden

jungles. They scaled the highest mountain for God and swam the widest oceans. They stood firm against all risks and dangers the world could ever afford them. Many among them sealed their glorious call to God's list of Generals with their blood. Their names glister on the pages of martyrs for Jesus and His course.

The greatest cry in the heart of God today is that He needs members of His inner circle. Will you be part of it or remain outside? Will you be one of God's Generals? Will you like to become a member of the Council of God? You are the person God has been looking for day and night. What testimony will you leave behind after your sojourn on earth?

Read this strange testimony.

A family lost its children, a total of thirteen babies. They were lost, usually after three, four, or six months of birth. The Spirit of God prompted a man of God, a father in the Lord and God's General to visit the bereaved family. This time the family just had another baby of three months. But the baby also was lost like others, making the mortality figure to become fourteen. This was quite unknown to the man of God on a visit to the family. As he was about to step into the house, he saw a woman of between thirty and thirty-two years of age, running out of the house naked.

The man of God thought there was a scuttle inside. He held this lady, trying to lead her back into the house to settle the quarrels. As soon as he held the lady, trouble started. He lost his voice immediately. The woman was speechless, and the man of God was unable to talk. He held on to her still, until people came and noticed she was trying to hide her face. The lady was dragged inside and to the utter dismay of everybody, she was the baby that just died. She confessed to have been the source of the sorrow in that family. She advised that the baby should be taken to another room that it would live; and it happened accordingly. That child that was revived is married now. The child survived because a 32- year- old lady came out of her.

A lot of strange things are happening around us nowadays. There is urgent need to go higher spiritually, otherwise it will become impossible to withstand these powers. There are a lot of strange news and stories that make the ears tingle nowadays.

A man and his wife were quarrelling. It got so serious one day that the woman hit the head of the man with an object and blood started flowing. In complete anger and revenge, the man got a knife and drove it into the woman. His surprise was that, though the knife penetrated the woman, there was no blood coming out. The man was amazed! He queried the woman why she had no blood in her body.

That's one of the strange things happening around. God is looking for people who will curtail the outbreak of wickedness and keep them where they belong. The world is waiting for the manifestation of the sons of God according to the Bible. I pray that whatever is preventing you from manifesting as a General in the army of the Lord, will die, in the name of Jesus.

If you want to be God's General, He has called you to become, you will be drawn into a life of crucifixion. He will put you on a very cross, and nail you there permanently.

Another thing that you cannot escape if God has called you into that life is humility. He will plunge you into a humble life. Humility will clothe you like a garment. He will put on you serious demands of obedience. Your life will be programmed divinely. God will make it impossible for you to follow other people, or measure yourself by other Christians. If He has called you into that inner circle, He will disallow you from doing many things He does not bother others about.

Others may be seeking pre-eminence wherever they are; you cannot do that because you belong to His inner circle.

Others may despise protocols to get what they want, you cannot because you belong to His inner circle.

Others may be scheming and manipulating to get ahead, members of the inner circle cannot.

If you attempt to do what others do, you will experience the kind of failure they do not experience and God will give you strong rebukes that will demolish you completely.

Others may be careless with the opposite sex, but you cannot because of the restrictions of the inner circle.

Others may be sleeping around, aborting pregnancies, you cannot because of the demands of the inner circle life. If you attempt it, you will almost die in the process.

Others may be involved in all kinds of sexual pervasion: oral sex, annal sex, lesbianism, masturbation, homosexuality etc, but you cannot. If you venture into any of those, all your heavenly visions and dreams will just vanish.

Others may be stealing from God's money but you cannot because you cannot lay the hand with which you steal on the dead, expecting the dead to rise. You cannot lay it on the sick, expecting recovery.

Others may be smoking and drinking secretly, you cannot because you belong to the inner circle.

Others may be addicted to the worldliness of painting of lips and nails, wearing of jewelleries and all other forms of adornment; but you cannot because you are a General in the army of God.

Others may require the interventions of in-laws and friends to be settling dispute between them and their spouses; but you cannot because you are higher than that.

You cannot boast like others, except you are boasting of what God can do. You cannot boast of your works like others, because you belong to the inner circle of God. You cannot talk about or praise your successes like others, because it is forbidden for members of the inner circle.

You are under heavy restrictions by the Holy Ghost from doing such things. If you force yourself to do it, you will suffer the rebuke of the Spirit that your life will become loathsome to you. The reason is because you belong to God's inner circle.

Others may abandon their spiritual lives to pursue wealth but you cannot. You brought nothing into the world and you will take nothing out of the world. As a General, God wants to supply your day to day needs, from His unseen treasury. For this reason, you cannot steal, cheat or defraud.

God can allow others to be praised and exalted by men and He will hide you somewhere. As a General, He is preparing you for the coming glory.

Others may be allowed to be great, while God is still working on your life like a technician. It is to enable you to explode at the fulness of time. He may let others get all the credit while you are denied. You do not fret over such things because as a General, your value is determined by God. He may even allow others to get the credit for all you have done! That does not make a General in the army of God get worried. It s just to make your reward ten times more at Jesus' return.

Others may spend all their income on things to outwardly beautify them, you cannot because your beauty is the glory of God. Of course if God had wanted all the elements of worldly adornments on you, He would have made provision for them right from your mother's womb. Others may find pleasure in adultery, you cannot, if you do not want to be demoted by the God who appointed you as a soldier.

Hypocrisy may be a game others find comfortable to play. You cannot do so because your two feet have been planted to run divine errands. Therefore, you cannot be one leg in or one leg out.

Others may be sitting on the fence. You cannot, because if you do, you will drop dead.

Others may be dressing to kill, but you cannot because your own dressing is consisted in the armour of God. There is no point to dress and kill physically, when inside you are naked.

Others may attach marine properties to their hair in whatever name of hair style or fixing; you cannot because your hair is the glory of God.

Others may marry outside the church, without bride price, engagements and other rites preceding holy marriage. You cannot, because you represent heaven on earth here.

Others may despise and disrespect their fathers and elders in the Lord. You cannot, because the word of God enjoins you to "honour your father and mother that your days may be long on earth." The opposite of this is that your days will be short if you do otherwise.

Others may be seeking worldly approval, you cannot, because what you need is the approval of heaven.

Others may be playing spiritual bats, neither a bird nor a rat. You cannot, because bats do not become Generals. You may disguise your appearance in the church and look different outside, you are a bat because you are neither here nor there.

Others may be comfortable without the Spirit's baptism. You cannot feel the same way, because you will be uncomfortable without the power of God to make you great.

Others may be comfortable without any gift of the Spirit: prophecy, word of knowledge, word of wisdom, miracles etc. none is found in such lives. The dreams they have are useless. You cannot afford to live like that because you'll become a trunkless elephant and an armless soldier.

Some people may be comfortable just attending services on Sundays alone. You cannot, because your well will run dry if you do the same.

Others may be patronising academic and other prostitutes, you cannot, because you will mortgage your anointing on the altar of Jezebel.

Other ladies may be comfortable with strange and defiled fingers running over their bodies, but you cannot take that, because you belong to God's inner circle.

Others may rush to marry unbelievers. You cannot, because you will be casting your pearls before swine.

Others may be doing what they like, but you cannot do so any more, because your life is no longer yours and the destinies of millions of people are attached to yours. If you fail, they will all fail. If you fail to acquire the volume of power God desires of you, a lot of people will fall into destruction without a rescue. By the time you appear at the throne of grace, a lot of blood will be crying against you.

God will accept you, once you decide to be close to Him. Once your training begins, the Holy Spirit will put a strict watch over your life. He will guard you with a jealous love. He will consider it an insult to share you with another. The Holy Spirit will rebuke you sharply for little unpleasant words or remarks. He will harass you over the least things other Christians do, even much more, without the slightest caution.

The Spirit will check you when you are doing what you ought not. These things may be things other Christians do and are not disturbed about them. Once He draws you close into that inner circle, God will not excuse you for sins others commit without caution. There are sins others commit that God overlooks. But if you attempt any of these, He will deal with you with a harsh hand.

The consequence of belonging to God's inner circle is grave. "Others may, but I cannot" will become your watchword in every thing.

Having agreed to belong to His inner circle, God will deal with you as He pleases. He may not explain to you now a thousand things happening to you at the moment, but He will explain to you later on.

When God is dealing with you in this special way, the Holy Spirit has the right to bind your tongue so that you cannot talk as you please. The Holy Spirit will not only forbid your tongue from your wishful uses, but He will also bind your hands. He has the right to close your eyes. He has the right to control you in the way He does not seem to want to control others. That is the reason you should not compare yourself with people. He will exhibit personal, peculiar jealousy over you. He will exercise aggressive management over your life.

If what you have read so far sounds strange to you, you are comparable to a PhD holder who saw a preacher in the market preaching on how all men, since Adam, are dead in sins and trespasses. The preacher went on to talk about how sinners are carrying heavy loads of sin and that they need relief through Jesus.

This learned man found the preaching unrealistic. He argued that after all, he could not feel the weight of any load on his head. The preacher responded and asked him if a dead man could feel any weight of any load on his head even if the world was laid on him. The erudite man said it is not possible for a dead person to feel anything. The preacher drove his point home by pointing it to him that because the doctor of philosophy was dead in sins and trespasses, he could not feel anything. That's the true state of every sinner.

Let me ask you some questions as we come to the end of this chapter.

Are you living as God planned for you? Is your heart right with God? Are you ready to give up all things for the sake of Jesus? Do you hold anything against anybody?

Do you live a double standard of life? Are you a stumbling block to the real children of God? Are you indulged in secret sins and pretending to be righteous?

If you want to belong to God's inner circle, you cannot afford to do any of the above. God can be close to you as He was to Noah, Joseph, Daniel, Moses, Abraham and others.

Will you be a General in this generation?

You have been set up as a watchman for your family. It will be a tragedy if you fail in your mission. The husbandman will not hesitate to cut down any unprofitable and fruitless tree in His garden.

Beware!

If you really want to be a friend of God, you need to re-order your life. Set your house in order and make your ways right with him. Your life is going on record before God. You may be nearer hell than you think.

PRAYER POINTS

1   Every conspiracy against my destiny in the heavenlies, scatter, in the name of Jesus.

2   Arrows of backwardness targeted against me this year, backfire, in the name of Jesus.

3   My destiny, arise by fire and reject disgrace, in the name of Jesus.

4   Every satanic vigil organised against my progress, scatter, in the name of Jesus.

5   Mark of tragedy, die, mark of breakthrough come, in the name of Jesus.

6   Walls of fire envelope me and my family, in the name of Jesus.

7   I shall arise and shine, no power shall put me down, in the name of Jesus.

8   Every power making my vision dark, die, in the name of Jesus.

9   O heavens over my spiritual vision, open by fire, in the name of Jesus.

CHAPTER 3

THE SON OF PERDITION

The subject in this chapter is a very serious matter. Perdition is not a word to commonly use because it has to do with the eternal damnation of a soul. But the Bible talks about the son of perdition. In fact, Jesus was the first person to use the expression "the son of perdition." He used it to describe the fate of Judas Iscariot. This man, who was once a disciple and an apostle of Christ, suffered the tragedy of eternal fire.

You may be a Christian reading this book. Do not be deceived by anything that your status as a child of God automatically insures you from the horror of perdition. There is no such thing as eternal security. Your salvation is conditional upon your keeping yourself from sinning.

Judas Iscariot was more than just a Christian. He was a disciple who had a record of having forsaken all like others. He was an apostle. He had the privilege of personal relationship with the Son of God. This man was among the privileged twelve appointed by Christ to belong to an inner circle of partnership and fellowship with Him. Upon all these, he became the son of perdition.

Perdition is an irreversible fate. You make yourself a son of perdition by stubbornly treading the path of ruin. When you damn the consequences of sin, despise God's eternal salvation, you are registering your name in the record of perdition. Perdition is eternal doom. It is becoming abandoned forever to the confines of divine wrath.

Whether you are a Christian or a sinner, this subject is most timely for your soul. If you are a Christian worker, remember Judas was one. If you have anointing, remember he was personally anointed by Christ. If you have a ministry, remember he was directly commissioned by Jesus.

If Judas became a son of perdition against whom the door of eternal mercies was closed, do not ever think yourself more highly than you ought.

If you are a sinner, you are even standing a more fearful ground of eternal punishment. Repentance and consistent righteous living is the answer to not becoming a son of perdition.

A son of perdition will keep moving on in the path of sin. A son of perdition will dine with Christ and keep in touch with the council of sinners. A child of perdition will be sinning secretly and pretending to be righteous among brethren. A child of perdition is a betrayer. A child of perdition will sell his salvation for money, position, honour or worldly gains.

A child of perdition will save souls, heal the sick, minister deliverance and still end up in hell. A child of perdition will only look for mercy when the door is forever closed. A child of perdition will both lose the gains of his compromises and his soul in hell. A child of perdition is destined to spend eternity in hell by his own choice.

Read the words of Jesus below.

John 17:12: While I was with them in the world, I kept them in thy name: those that thou gavest me I have kept, and none of them is lost, but the son of perdition; that the scripture might be fulfilled.

Jesus kept all the other disciples but lost one: the son of perdition. The son of perdition got lost right from the armpit of God. He got lost from under the direct guide of Christ. Getting lost under the shadow of God's wings is a terrifying thing. Getting lost, despite divine protection, is fearful. Divine provision and privileges are a waste to the son of perdition.

In the historic prayer of Jesus, He said He lost none but the son of perdition. He tried to keep all, but still lost the son of perdition. He taught all, but still lost the son of perdition.

The son of perdition will perish despite everything done to save him. The son of perdition will go to hell despite efforts to make him go to heaven. The son of perdition will sit with other believers, pray with them, work with other Christian workers, live under the leadership of the same master, learn the same tradition of the church, yet he will go to hell.

Read another text below.

2 Thess. 2:3: Let no man deceive you by any means: for [that day shall not come], except there come a falling away first, and that man of sin be revealed, the son of perdition;

Different titles are ascribed to the same person in this text. Before it finally borrows the words of Jesus to call him the son of perdition, he is first described as the man of sin. His coming, presence will be announced by a falling away. This means a falling from grace. Join the text above to the one below, you will get a clearer picture of the destiny of the son of perdition.

Heb. 10:39: But we are not of them who draw back unto perdition; but of them that believe to the saving of the soul.

There is a drawing back leading to perdition. There is a falling away leading to sin. There is a drawing back from grace leading to doom. There is a forsaking of God leading to hell. There is a despise of Jesus leading to eternal punishment.

What is your position to Christ now? How far or near are you from Him? Have you appropriated His promises?

Check your relative position to the Master. Maybe you have already commenced the journey to perdition.

Acts 1:17: For he was numbered with us, and had obtained part of this ministry.

Judas Iscariot was numbered with the ministry of witnessing the life of Christ in the private or in the open. But his lot was replaced and another took his place. His ministry was given to another and his position was taken away from the book of life.

Acts 1:20: For it is written in the book of Psalms, Let his habitation be desolate, and let no man dwell therein: and his bishoprick let another take.

The son of perdition is a betrayal of his Master. Jesus said of Himself at His betrayal, that the Son of man goes as it is written of Him, but woe to the man by whom He is betrayed. It would have been better for him not to have been born. In order words, Jesus said it is even better to be childless than to have a son or a daughter of perdition.

A man of God had a revelation some years ago. He slept that night and God said to him, "Oh, I want to take you to a place," and he told God he was ready. God took him up and he saw heaven and its beauty. He did not want to come, back but the Lord told him he had not seen all he should see. There was another thing for him to see. He was taken to another place where he saw hell fire. He saw fire entering into the nostrils of men and women and coming out like breath. He saw fire like worms, entering and coming out. He saw men and women crying, rolling and groaning in big time lamentations. He saw many members of his church that had been dead and buried, but are groaning in hell. He considered the suffering on their faces and broke down crying.

He determined not to be part of them that would spend eternity in hell. Then the Lord said to him: "Son, do you know why most of these people are here?" He replied that it must be because they were living in sin. But God said that was not correct, that they went to hell for three major reasons.

That is how they do it syndrome: Following the way and tradition of multitudes will lead to hell.

It does not matter: What is so serious about this?

They knew the truth too late.

He was told that these are the three things that took them to hell. Hell fire is the truth known too late! If you don't know the truth about the salvation of your soul, you may have signed the pact with doom. If you don't accept the truth you have known now, you may have entered into agreement with eternity in hell.

I always pray that anyone who wants to be a pastor or serve God should first be shown the picture of heaven and the horror of hell, before being thrown into the field of service. That man will preach like a mad man after seeing those things.

The reason some are playing with things of eternal

gravity is because they have not seen the vision of heaven and hell. The reason some are watching the magic of the serpent is because they have not seen the picture of heaven and hell.

If you see heaven and hell, the glory of the world will fade away in your sight. What people value and pursue eagerly will lose its hold on you. You will come to grips with the Scriptures that say "All is vanity upon vanity, all is vanity."

You were once urgent about marriage and now you have a husband, but your face is now a punching bag. Vanity of vanities, all is vanity.

You cried that you wanted children. God has given them to you and now you are the witch spoiling your own family.

You wanted a car. You got it at last and later lost it to armed robbers.

You craved for money but if when it comes, you never live to enjoy it, what happens? Your children may even be fighting over another over it.

Now that you have got the certificate you craved so eagerly for, what happens? It is vanity of vanities, all is vanity.

You need the enlightenment of the Scriptures and you will have a change of attitude. The way people live, pushing and shoving, shouting and screaming at bus stops and in commercial buses, show that something is behind it. And when you see preachers of the gospel sweating and shouting, giving out the word of God, something is behind it. That is the reason one of my favourite passages in the Scriptures is "Go and preach the gospel."

Paul, the apostle, said "I have nothing to glory of, but necessity is laid upon me." I am worried if I preach not the gospel. He went further and said "Woe is me if I preach not the gospel." That is the language of the men who have seen the pictures of the two camps: heaven and hell.

What is perdition? It is ruin, loss, destruction and condemnation. It means eternal death and punishment. It is the opposite of salvation. It is the final stage of complete ruin.

To describe someone as a son of perdition is very horrible. The expression 'son of perdition' is only used to describe two persons in the Bible: Judas Iscariot and the anti-christ. The account of Judas Iscariot has been read in John Chapter seventeen verse twelve, and that of the anti-christ in second Thessalonians chapter two verse three. A little focus on the life of Judas will give you a clearer picture of a son of perdition.

Jesus prayed all night to have him numbered with the twelve. He enjoyed the authority and title of an apostle. Even when he was on the path of doom, the Master was still in prayer to get him out. Somebody may have interceded for you to be saved. Your remaining in the

Lord may be as a result of someone else's prayer. But the Scripture warns, "He that thinketh he standeth, let him take heed, lest he falls." You don't hold a golden coin in your hand in a canoe and you start tossing it up and down. If you do that, you are planning to lose it.

Judas was chosen after prayers. He was sent out as one of the twelve to whom Jesus said, "Behold, I give unto you, power to tread upon serpents and scorpions." When the work expanded and Jesus sent His disciples out in twos, Judas was among. He went out with others to heal the sick, raise the dead, cleanse the lepers, and preach the gospel.

Many of the Christians of today are very far from the mark of Judas in working miracles, signs and wonders. Before he went to perdition, Judas got to a point many of us are yet to reach today.

This man Judas was accompanying Jesus around. He was beholding the character and power of Jesus. He heard Jesus teach. He heard Him say He is the Messiah to come. With all he saw and experienced, he never came to full faith with the Messiah.

When the enemy finally schemed to destroy him, he was made the treasurer of Jesus' ministry. He was in charge of money. You need to be careful so that the position you are given will not ruin you. Your leadership position may close the gate of heaven against you. You need to apply serious caution.

You are the mother- in- Israel, mother- in- Judah, Egypt and so on. That title may be what will close the gate of heaven against you. Your claim of pre- eminence in ministry may be what will close the gate of heaven against you.

This man, Judas, was put in charge of money. The devil is an expert planner. He was put in charge of what eventually ruined him.

I sent somebody somewhere to go and minister, and someone wrote from there and said he should be cautioned because all his counselees are women.

The enemy has a way of pursuing one. He will concentrate on where he knows you will somersault. He did it to Judas. Judas was the one complaining that the ointment of oil was being wasted on the feet of Jesus. He said that as if he cared for the poor, whereas he was demonstrating his covetous spirit.

When Jesus entered into Jerusalem with the shout of Hosanna and the shout of praises, the Pharisees were envious and wanted to destroy him. The same Pharisees wanted to kill Lazarus because they found out that he kept his testimonies that Jesus is the son of God. In their plan to get Jesus, they needed a medium. Judas presented himself before them with a proposal. He began to look for a way to betray Jesus. The master did everything to prevent him from entering into this bondage.

When they sat at super Jesus said, "One of you will betray me tonight." The disciples felt concerned. And they started asking one after the other: "Master, is it I?" When it got to the turn of Judas, Jesus did not hesitate to tell him that he was the betrayer. That was enough for him to caution himself. But he accepted that pronouncement and satan entered into him.

I want you to know that the devil entered into this man right in the presence of Jesus. He went ahead with his compromise to betray the Son of God and perfected the act with a kiss. After Jesus was arrested, he began to regret his action. He took the money back to them that hired his service. His repentance and restitution were too late. They simply told him that the deal was over. They have got who they wanted.

He betrayed the Son of man with a kiss. He lost the gains of the bargain by throwing the money away. His journey to perdition ended when he hanged himself. He later opened his eyes in the lake of fire to reap the eternal reward of his betrayed.

Compromises may be sweet, but the agonies of hell are terrible. The pleasure of this world may be enjoyable but the pains of hell are unending.

You may be betraying the Master in your business endeavours, pursuit of career, activities in the church and so on; one day, the Lord will repay everyone according to his works.

The money Judas threw away was used to purchase a burial ground. He lost his money. He also lost his soul. The deceit of the devil is very clear. Whatever he is presenting to you now will only make you a son of perdition. You will lose the gift as well as lose your soul.

You have just read a brief account of Judas, the first human being to be called the son of perdition.

What do you learn from these? Judas was of a tribe close to Jesus. He knew Jesus personally. He spent years working and travelling with Jesus. But he lacked honesty with money. Therefore, the enemy was able to pick him as the best available candidate for a mission of betrayal. All the power and authority he had exercised in the past were no longer of any significance. His record before God was wiped away. His name was changed from the register of life to death, that is why your primary aim should be how to get to heaven. You only get reward for your labour if only you get to heaven at last. Judas was probably the greatest Bible example of a wasted opportunity and destiny.

The name Judas is so synonymous with shame that nobody wants to name his child after Judas Iscariot. If he had not done what he did, the Bible would probably have had a Gospel according to saint Judas. All that is left in his memorial is a field of blood.

There are many sons and daughters of perdition in the world today. Unfortunately, sons and daughters of perdition are also in the church today. Some people do not even want Jesus to come now because they know they are not ready. But Jesus will come at the time unknown to any human.

Who is a child of perdition? They are the chosen but the unsaved. A mere look at you, that reveals the spiritual aura of a chorister, house fellowship leader, a preacher, a pastor, a woman leader, etc. is an evidence that you have been chosen. But if you have not been saved, you are a child of perdition.

A child of perdition is one who has been chosen but prefers to be a vessel unto dishonour.

A child of perdition is an unsaved miracle worker, a pastor, a minister, a deliverance minister etc. If you look at the Bible of some pastors, instead of tracts, you find complimentary cards of business men. Look at the telephone directory of many pastors, what you find are lines where they can make money.

A child of perdition is someone who is holding a very important position in the church but is very far from heaven. Those singing and talking about heaven but are far from there are children of perdition. You sing that nobody should bother to look for you in Egypt, whereas Egypt is really your home. You are a child of perdition.

A child of perdition is one who takes after the examples of backsliders. He backslides because others backslide. He continues in his stumbling on the high way to doom.

A child of perdition is the strong tree in the house of God that is already falling but still seemingly standing.

Who is a child of perdition?

He is someone, who in the record of heaven is a star of the morning but has dropped from the gate of heaven. What happened to the spirit of prophecy that used to be upon you? Who stole it away from your life? What are you doing to repossess these things? If you are not doing anything about them you are a child of perdition.

A child of perdition is a lost coin in the house of God.

The Bible talks about three lost items. One, lost sheep. Two, a lost coin. Three, the prodigal son. It is easy to find a lost sheep because of its bleating in the street. This represents the unbelievers afflicted by the devil in the world.

But when somebody is a lost coin, it is very difficult to recover. A coin can be lost in a room for a year without recovery. You can sweep the room, and yet your broom does not touch the coin. Many are in the church, lost within the church. They have disappeared before God. They are disobedient to God. They have forsaken God. They have lost their orientation. They are lost coins.

I am concerned about actors and pretenders in the house of God because the fire and the power of God's judgement will find them out. If you don't repent and the lots of the son of perdition comes upon you, the Bible says it is better you had not been born.

A child of perdition is someone with a light of God but abuses divine opportunities and privileges. Opportunities determine responsibility.

If you are beating your spouse, you are a child of perdition. If you are under the shadow of God and you are abusing the privileges, you are a child of perdition.

A child of perdition is someone brought up with exposure to the gospel but is not really a Christian. You have been attending Sunday School since you were a child as a lady, but now you go about in immoral affairs with men. You are a daughter of perdition.

I had a strange visitor in my counselling room sometime ago. He was a 68- year- old bishop. He got into my office and sat down. When I asked him what he needed, he said he wanted me to pray for him and give him prayer points to destroy his wife. I asked him why. He said because his wife was a bloody witch. I asked him what really happened and he said his wife made a pronouncement against him that rendered him impotent. He said the woman did it to forestall his immorality.

She had once caught him with his secretary in immoral relationship in the office. I gave him a very hard counsel that was thought provoking. I warned him to beware, because he was already becoming a son of perdition.

His experience shows that when he became a pastor,

he was a pastor of perdition. When he became a bishop, he was a bishop of perdition. At sixty- eight, he was still on that path of perdition. That is the reason the Bible says "He that thinketh he standeth should take heed, lest he falls." Your life is open before God.

There was the story of a man who went into another man's farm to steal. He instructed his little girl to keep watch to alert him by whistling if anybody was coming. As he continued in his trespass, the girl whistled once and said somebody was looking at them. The father did not see anybody. The girl did the same the second and the third time to the annoyance of her father who did not see anybody watching them. At last, the girl pointed to heaven and said that is where the person looking at us is. God is looking at you. In the day of your death, you will meet with the awful reality of eternity.

Who is a son of perdition?

He is the one with all spiritual advantages but never cares about the things of God. Those that make choices that lead them to perdition are children of perdition. They never knew that sin does not deliver what it promises.

Children of perdition are those who co- operate with satan. A woman called me on the phone one day, crying bitterly, she wanted me to help her. Her Problem? She introduced herself as a contractor who had promised God never to sleep with anybody again in the process of getting contracts. She was so resolute about this that she told God if she ever did that again, God should kill her.

She wanted me to pray when she had failed in fulfilling her promise.

Somebody associated with Christ but not truly saved is a child of perdition. There are ushers of perdition; there are choristers of perdition; there are pastors of perdition.

Children of perdition are those who climb every obstacle God puts on their ways to prevent them from sinning. They break through all the barriers of God to hold them back from sin.

Those that feel sorry without repenting are children of perdition.

Judas had a ministry but no repentance. He had a service but no salvation. Many criminals in the prisons today are sad not because they are repentant but because they are caught. If Jesus has been knocking on your door and you refuse to open, you are a child of perdition.

Those who are just seeking the hands of Jesus and not His face, are children of perdition. They are concerned with what they can receive from Him.

Who is a son of perdition?

He is the one who rejects the correction of the Holy Spirit. If you continue to despise the gentle warnings of the Holy Spirit, a time will come when He will talk to you no more! At that point, perdition has set in.

A son of perdition will sit under the ministrations of the most anointed teachers preachers yet, he leaves untouched and unmoved.

Those who have stopped serving God and are angry with Him are children of perdition. They take offence against God because He has not done as they expected.

Somebody who never broke down to cry over his or her sin is a child of perdition.

Children of perdition are those persons who are greedy for money. They are serving God for money. They sing praises and worship but they do not pray. Their worship is not from the heart. They have little or no contact with God after leaving the services. Some come to church when they want to, they read their Bibles in order to preach to others; such are children of perdition.

If you are worshipping in a Bible believing church but your parents cannot see the changes in your life, you are still angry, worldly, etc. you should be assured that right on the corridor of the promised land, you are already an agent of perdition.

There is a place for weeping and gnashing of teeth. There is a place known as the bottomless pit. There is a place known as outer darkness. There is a place known as a place of sorrow. There is a place, where the fire is never quenched, where there is no rest, day or night. There is a place, where the worms die not. There is a place of everlasting destruction. There is a place of bad memory and regret. There is a place of hopelessness and suffering. That is the place where the children of perdition will end up.

Beloved, you need to be more serious. About one hundred and twenty thousand people die every minute. Ninety-nine percent of these people go to hell fire. Yet, the Scriptures say hell has enlarged itself to take some more.

A child of perdition will perish like the Israelites in the wilderness. Though, the pillars of fire and the cloud were protecting them. They were moving in the wilderness but wasting away. It was a very terrible experience they had.

You need to cry out to the Lord that you do not want your lot to be like that. These Israelites were already under the curse of wastage. God had pronounced on them that they were going to perish in the wilderness. Their journey was monitored by a divine curse.

In spite of the fact that God had pronounced wastage on them, He was still protecting them. They were still eating manner from heaven. He was still providing for them. He was still defending them. Miracles, signs and wonders were still happening in their midst. Their case is like buying a Christmas goat, and the goat is being fed from June for the purpose of slaughter in December. The goat might be growing fat and fresh as a result of this, but at Christmas, death is awaiting it. At Christmas, it will say its last prayer. All what the owner cares about is to find an end in the slaughtering of the goat.

This is a very crucial moment. You need to examine

your life. Are you a child of perdition? Where do you stand? Where do you belong? If your name is not written in the book of life, already you are a child of perdition. But you can repent today. If you have been a hypocrite in the church, you are on the path of doom; but you can repent today; you have stayed long enough away from the love, the grace, and the power of Christ.

Make this moment a turning point in your life. Hell is real and Heaven is real. Where will you spend eternity? Go before the Lord in prayer. Pour out your heart to Him. Cry out mightily and bitterly for Him to rescue your soul. Accept the redemption by the blood of Jesus. Surrender your life completely to Jesus as your Lord and saviour.

PRAYER POINTS

1   My Father, I have failed You, help me today, in the name of Jesus.

2   Satanic vision, die, in the name of Jesus.

3   Heavenly vision appear, in the name of Jesus

4   Every power of iniquity of my father's house, die, by the blood of Jesus.

5   I shall not drop back into perdition, in the name of Jesus Christ

6   Blood of Jesus purge my sins away, in the mighty name of Jesus.

CHAPTER 4

THE SHRINE OF SELF

Self is one of the greatest enemies of the believer. Every sincere Christian needs to pray very hard to deal with it. As you read this chapter, you will need to pray this prayer point immediately.

My Father, dig deep into my life, in the name of Jesus.

You can only know the true nature and operations of self through the revelations of God. That is why the prayer you just prayed is very important. Until God reveals your self to you, you may be ignorantly operating by its dictates.

Self has the tendency to operate independently of God's bidding. The potential in a man to live and do things in ways other than by the will of God is a manifestation of self. You will discover more about it as you read.

Shrines are a familiar phenomenon to Africans because they are common in every community. A shrine is a place of worship of gods and idols. A shrine is a contact point between men and demons, principalities and powers.

God is in the business of disqualifying men and women when they fail to meet His standard. The reason is because there is a personal shrine in every life where men and women worship. This shrine is self.

You will immediately discover the operations of self when it is confronted by the will of God on any matter. Self would want to have its way or do the will of God by its own method. The most difficult thing in life is for anyone to know himself or herself in the true sense of it. Oftentimes, people have a wrong conception of their real selves. They are not what they think they are. They manifest certain traits and exhibit certain attitudes to their own surprise.

Self can be so hidden in a man that he feels it is not there. One of the easiest ways to expose it is to set the will of God and the way of God as top priority. You will suddenly discover an entity within that has a different agenda. As the most difficult thing in life is for anyone to know himself, so also the easiest person to deceive is oneself. The worst injustice and fraud anybody can ever perpetrate is for a man to deceive himself.

The tragedy of this truth is that some know very well that they are deceiving themselves. They are convinced of this within them. They need no preacher to tell them that they are not on the way to heaven at all; yet they pretend about it.

A head usher of a church came to me for prayer. He was restless because of God's dealings with him. He noticed that the pastor of his church was stealing from the offering without suffering any consequences he could see. This pastor would rake all the ₦50.00 notes from the offerings into his pocket. The usher thought he would fall down and die one day, but he did not; instead, the man was growing fatter.

Comparing himself with the pastor, he therefore decided to do the same. So, as the pastor was taking the ₦50.00 notes, he too was taking the ₦20.00 notes. But the first day he did that, an angel of God appeared to him in a dream and told him that for what he did, his generations unborn would suffer the consequences.

Surprised, he tried to excuse himself before the angel by pointing to the pastor's much longer experiences in the act. The angel told him that the pastor was a temporary staff in the service of God but that he was supposed to carry the power of God for many years. What pushed this man to the dirty deal was the shrine of self.

If for example in a church, the bags of all the brothers and sisters were ransacked, it would be frightening to discover that ninety nine percent of their contents are items to worship self. You would find combs to keep the hair of the shrine of self, mirrors to look at the shrine very well, lipsticks to paint the lips of the shrine in colours desired, and last of all, a small copy of the Bible, pushed to a corner somewhere in the bags.

If you want more of Christ in you, that Christ may increase abundantly in your life, there must be a decrease of self as a consequence. The song writer knew what ought to be the desire of every believer and preacher when he wrote "More of Christ, more, more, more... ."

There is a truism in the saying that it is madness for anyone to increase his speed, when he has already missed his way. Flesh is the force that makes you run actively and zealously when your direction is absolutely wrong.

Of all the four-lettered words in the dictionary, the worst is self. Everybody is clamouring for a national and global change, but only a few are ready to change themselves. The will and commandment of God for you is very clear at this point. Lay aside the shrine of self or God Himself will lay you aside. Stop comparing and contrasting yourself with another because the Bible says: "The battle is not for the strong and the race is not for the swift." God has an agenda for your life.

I was living in a police barracks during my secondary school days. There was a playing field in the barracks where I had opportunity to train myself in running and also contacted some aggression from watching the police train. I was to represent my house in a race competition.

On the competition day, we all got ready and took off at the shot of the gun. That first attempt was cancelled because I was told that I had jumped the gun. I was, forthwith, threatened that if that happened again, I would be completely disqualified. The threat weakened my zeal, unknown to me that it was deliberate because I had been marked out as an athlete to watch, who was sure to win the race.

Eventually when the race took off, the other competitors outran me and the race ended like that. The point is that it is not how well or fast you start a race, but how well you finish it.

Lay the shrine of self aside and let God use you. If you keep it to yourself, God will lay you aside and look for a replacement who is ready to lay self aside.

Make this confession loud and clear: "I live to die and I die to live. The more I die, the more I live."

What you have just said is why Paul said: " I die daily." The more the shrine of self dies in your life, the more of God rises up in your life. If you are desiring to be hearing God audibly, just let self die. As long as you let it live, God is not interested in you at all.

The flesh is your greatest predicament. The flesh is your greatest enemy. Your greatest enemy is not the devil or witches and wizards, but the shrine you carry about. The temptations of satan against you are only effective because of your sinful nature. The sin in you welcomes the temptations, which in turn, cause troubles for you.

Demons will see you and run immediately you are able to put flesh where it belongs. For demons to operate in your life, they need a small ladder of the shrine of self, to come in.

A man once believed the whole world was his enemy because of his experiences. He lost his job five times, his wife ran away, somebody impregnated his first daughter in secondary school. He was depressed. He therefore cried out to God in all desperation and pleaded with God to intervene in his life.

Do you know that you can pray to a level when heavenly beings will appear to you and converse with you clearly and audibly? So, this man prayed and the Lord appeared to him. He was very happy, because he wanted the Lord to sympathise with him, promote him, give him deliverance from all his troubles and kill all those making life difficult for him. He wanted fairness, understanding and justice from the Lord.

To the amazement of this man, the Lord sternly pointed

at him and told him that his problem was rooted in him and not in those perceived enemies. "This is the hardest part of the Christian life. You are yet to agree that you are your own problem. Son, you are only deceiving yourself by blaming the devil. Son, listen to Me and listen to Me very well. I am the Almighty. I am not struggling with the devil. I desire that your flesh should be in subjection to My Spirit. I want to dethrone you from the centre of your life and be your Lord. You must strife to contend with your flesh because it does more to hinder My work than any evil spirit you have been praying against. Son, the devil is not the issue as much as the power of your flesh," the Lord told him.

He was dazed, because he had thought the Lord would promise him victory over the enemies and fight against them but instead, the Lord told him that he was the greatest enemy of his life because of the reign of self. In the same vein, you are the problem of your life. You are the one opening the door for the enemies to come in. Your toughest battle is with the flesh.

Gal. 5:17: For the flesh lusteth against the Spirit, and the Spirit against the flesh: and these are contrary the one to the other: so that ye cannot do the things that ye would.

The battle between the flesh and the spirit is so serious that if the flesh is not subdued, you will not be able to fulfill your destiny. The flesh hinders you from doing what you desire in line with God's will. That is why fasting is one way of reducing the power of the flesh. When there is no food, the power of the flesh decreases. When the flesh becomes very weak, the spirit has the room to rise.   That is the secret of fasting. Fasting does not change God, but you.   During this exercise, you are able to pray more clearly, distinctly and get more results.

The battle is a ding-dong affair. When your spiritual life functions in a ding-dong manner, there is a problem. The day your flesh rises so high that your spirit is low, the enemy will come, plant evil in your life and take his leave. You now begin to pray. You open the door to the enemy through the uncrucified flesh. That is why people attend power-packed programmes, get the miracles but lose them when self sets in.   Some people lose their miracles at car packs or at home. It happens when they speak unadvisedly with their tongues after just receiving a great breakthrough or miracle from God.

The devil knows how to arrange for this. The flesh is not worried about your prayerfulness so long as it is not permanently crucified.   The slightest provocation may come from a child who carelessly left the burning pot of soup on the fire and played away. It may come from a fellow user of the road who drives recklessly to your hurt. When this happens, and you give in to the reaction of the flesh, you lose your miracle at once.

People engage in unprofitable conversations in the church instead of fervently praying for God's visitation and interceding for others. Though they are prompt to arrive for church meetings, they give the time to discussions that will either hinder their blessing or make them lose it.

There was a young man that was brought to us unconscious at the headquarters church. After prayers, he was revived and henceforth became well. Later in his conscious, normal self and sense, he started gossiping about a deliverance minister whom he considered too short in stature to marry his much taller fiancee. You wonder what his problem should be with such things if not for the force of the flesh, working to his ruin.

The devil knows the limit of his power. He knows the judgement pronounced against him from the beginning. He is only looking for opportunities to strike through the flesh. God pronounced on the devil that his food will be dust. You find that account in Genesis chapter three. But you and I know that serpents do not eat dust. The dust referred to here is the flesh! What the devil is looking for is an occasion through the flesh. Jesus said: "The prince of this world cometh and hath nothing in me." There was no place in the flesh of Jesus, where the devil could gain access.

Jesus was dead to Himself. He was dead to His desires. He was dead to His agenda. If as you are reading this book, you discover that you lose your defence at the sight of any man or woman, there is something in your flesh that must die.

Lust in the heart needs to die. If God had decided to use you, and the flesh is still reigning in your life, you will be disqualified or at best, become a temporary instrument. So, there are people that point others to the way of heaven and they do not walk in the way themselves.

There are spiritual touts that invite others to join the wagon to heaven, but they themselves have nowhere to go. Others work like a bill-board or a sign post that shows the way but does not move at all.

The powers of darkness have the best gadgets use to x-ray anybody or anything. Only a glance from their penetrating eyes, and they know the spiritual level of any believer. They know who is dangerous to them and who is not. They know who to obey and who not to obey. That is why when the six vagabond sons of Sceva commanded the spirit of divination in the name of Jesus whom Paul preached to leave its hosts, the spirit replied and said: "Paul I know, Jesus I know, but who are you?"

You can parade yourself as a General Overseer, a pastor, a prophet, a deliverance minister, a house fellowship leader, etc. but God knows your true spiritual state and position. The devil and his cohorts also do. You may be the best chorister, singing with miracles, signs and wonder following, it does not matter, when the powers of darkness scan your life, they know whether or not you have anointing, fire, power, etc.

I visited a branch of our church overseas. I was about to lead the congregation in a song when the Lord suddenly called my attention to the organist. He was a very handsome man. The Lord said concerning him that if I did not remove him from playing the organ as we set to sing, he was going to pollute the meeting. I called the pastor of the church and told him to remove the man.

After all, one of the earliest lessons to learn in doing God's business is obedience. Therefore, I made up my mind to do as God commanded. The host pastor felt it was unfair and embarrassing to remove the man. He was hired and had been payed by the church. I insisted and the church organist replaced him immediately, though not as skilful as the hired organist.

At the end of the service, he said he wanted to see me and when I gave him an audience, he demanded to know the reason he was embarrassed in the church. I looked at him and said: "When last did you visit a prostitute?" He replied: "Just before I came to this meeting." I then let him know that it was for the same reason he could not be allowed to play the piano. "Help me sir," he pleaded for spiritual assistance. There are many such people in the church, though they sing and play musical instruments beautifully, they are fake inside.

You may be in this category. Let me ask you a question. How long do you want to continue in your compromises? Will you not cry out to the Lord to deliver you at once? The scanning machine of the powers of darkness can detect the smallest compromise in your life. The powers of darkness can detect the minutest sin in the life of a man. That is why the prayer life of many lack potency and effectiveness. When they pray, these powers quieten them that after all, they belong to the same camp.

It is very sad that many do not understand this. When their flesh create room for the enemies to have a field day in their lives, they tend to magnify their problems, overlooking the flesh that is primarily the issue to address.

If you are a Christian with uncrucified flesh, the devil will defeat you with ease. Satan is looking for an accommodation to dwell in. He will readily take residence in any area of your life you fail to submit to God. Your life is like a big mansion. God will only accommodate the apartment you yield to Him and vacate to you the ones you don't.

What accounts for the absence and scarcity of God's power in this generation is the unavailability of yielded vessels. God is not to blame at all. Jesus is always at the door, knocking. Will you open the door to Him? Whatever part of your life you submit to the devil, he will use. He will use your hair, head, thought, marriage, ears, the mouth, eyes, jobs, ambition, certificates, voice, etc. Whatever you submit to him, he will use.

Look again at the text below.

Gal. 5:24: And they that are Christ's have crucified the flesh with the affections and lusts.

There are surgical prayers to pray as you read this book. There are things to be cut off from your life. You must get to a point you don't run away from temptations but they either run away from you or you are completely dead to them. You must get to a point you accept responsibilities for your shortcomings and cry out to God for deliverance.

The text is addressing those that belong to Christ, not just church goers. If you still harbour lusts, you are not yet of Christ. Peter was tempted with money when Simon the sorcerer offered him money to "buy" the power of God. But the great apostle promptly reacted: "Your money perish with you." Peter reacted this way because there was nothing in him to magnetise him to the temptation of money.

I have often shared this testimony about how our headquarters church started. There was only one auditorium then. Everywhere was swampy. Members of the congregation had to pull their shoes to wade through the swamp to enter in for worship. Some of our friends from high brow Ikoyi and Victoria Island were forced to tred the soil barefooted, for the first time in their lives. The piece of land we were using was bought for ₦120,000.00 (one hundred and twenty thousand naira) then, in 1993. That amount of money was very difficult to come by.

We purchased the land through the singular giving of a sister. It was really a time the church needed money desperately. A man came to me for prayers. He had money but couldn't sleep. He promised to give me two million naira if only I could pray for him so he could sleep. I looked at the man and told him: "You want to give me the money you have and yet, are unable to sleep? You want me to collect the money so that I too could lose my sleep?" He hadn't slept for six mouths. Well, I prayed for him but refused to take his money.

Another person came to my counselling room one day, with the key of a V-boot Mercedes Benz car. It was in the days the car was really in vogue. I looked at the man and discerned adultery in his life. I refused to accept his gift. I strongly counselled him to give his life to Christ, go through deliverance exercise, become absolutely broken and join the church as a member whose life could easily be assessed. I assured him that at that time, I could take any gift from him, but not while he is an unrepentant adulterer.

Christianity is not a child's play. Being a minister of God is even more exceedingly serious. If I had taken the gift, I might have muzzled the truth because the day I preach against his adultery, he would not hesitate to recover his car. I just let it be. He was surprised and went home with his car.

Don't allow self to reign in your life because of the immediate gratifications of worldly things. If for a morsel of meat you are ready to despise your salvation, you are not the kind of instrument God is looking for. Self in man does not care for the things of God, but for such things as appeal to it.

Look at the gifts you have received so far, what motivated you to accept them? Self or the express permission of God? There is nothing wrong in accepting a gift arranged by God. The problem with self is that it is ready to accept any gift for its pleasure without respect for its consequences on the things of God.

The enemy knows about the smallest unfaithfulness in your life. He can discern the smallest spot of lies in your life. You may tell a man of God lies and get away with it, but the truth is that satan knows you have told lies.

Peter had allowed God to crucify self in his life, therefore, it was quite easy for him to overcome the temptation of money. Crave for money is one area of life where self is reigning in people's lives.

The flesh enables man to engage in activities contrary to the Holy Spirit. The flesh cannot be improved upon. It is rotten to the core. Most of the problems Christians have are caused by the shrine of the flesh. Be it disobedience, rash decision, irrational thinking etc, the root of all is the flesh.

The most difficult thing for a man to face is himself. The flesh is very dangerous and merciless. It is harder to deal with than the devil.

There are four basic enemies a child of God has to contend with. The first is sin. That's why the Bible says: "For this cause the Son of God came to the world that He might redeem us from our sins." Jesus was born to take our sins away.

The second enemy is the world. The Bible tells us that, "In the world, ye shall have tribulation, but be of good cheer because I have overcome the world."

The third enemy is the devil. And God has recommended how to deal with him. The Bible says: "Resist the devil and he shall flee from you."

The fourth enemy is the flesh. It is one shrine that demands worship every day, every time, everywhere. God does not have a recommendation on how to manage the flesh.

There is nothing to manage in the flesh. The method of God is to put the operations of the flesh completely out of the way. The flesh cannot be renewed. It can never be born again. It is the body of sin and the capacity and tendency to sin in a man. Paul described it as the body of death. In his fierce battle against the flesh, he cried: " Who shall deliver me from this body of death?" He found all his efforts to manage the corruption and weaknesses of the flesh to have failed. No human being can improve on the flesh to redeem it from its nature. Paul found a solution to his "in Christ Jesus". Only the Lord can help you overcome the powers of the flesh.

The Bible condemns the flesh in very strong terms. Flesh as used here, puts together self and sin. Read the Bible passage below.

Rom. 6:6: Knowing this, that our old man is crucified with [him], that the body of sin might be destroyed, that henceforth we should not serve sin.

The flesh is called "our old man". Look at God's method of dealing with it. The answer is crucifixion. "Our old man is crucified." When you nail something to a tree somewhere, it remains there. This is God's way of putting the flesh and its operations out of the way. The man on the cross is helpless. He cannot come down to fight. He cannot accept any gift. He cannot commit immorality even if the most beautiful lady in the world stands naked before him. He cannot smoke like others. He cannot partake in any human activity as long as he is fastened to the cross.

Do you now see the need for a crucified life? People don't appreciate the message of crucifixion. Many abhor to live the crucified life. But this is one thing that accounted for the victory over the flesh, consequently over the world, sin and satan in the lives of Bible and contemporary heroes of faith. You must be crucified. You cannot manage the flesh. The solution is to experience crucifixion. The reason some people think they are holy is because they are yet to have the opportunity to sin. When nobody is watching you apart from God, how do you mange and live your life? For a crucified life, private or public life does not make any difference. The man on the cross cannot do anything whether in the open or in the private.

Let us look at another strong term the Bible uses to address the problem of the flesh. Read again in the book of Romans.

Rom. 6:6: Knowing this, that our old man is crucified with [him], that the body of sin might be destroyed, that henceforth we should not serve sin.

The description "our old man" is replaced with "the body of sin." It is all about the same thing. What follows the body of sin? Destruction! "That the body of sin might be destroyed, ..." is God's goal in your life. God cannot reign alongside sin or self in your life. He is working towards just one target; that the body of sin might be destroyed. He wants to incapacitate you to sin or be ruled by self.

Paul experienced these glorious workings of God to become the glorious apostle. "I am crucified with Christ..." he said. He experienced crucifixion of the flesh and self. Any wonder he did exploits for God in all strict righteousness and holy living. Because self had been dethroned in him and the body of sin incapacitated, he could therefore "keep his body under" where it should belong.

Death is another word God uses to describe His verdict on our self and sin. You must die to yourself and die to sin because: "He that is dead is freed from sin" (Rom. 6:7). When you die to self and sin, you begin to enjoy the liberty of Jesus Christ. If you allow God to work this out in your life, then "sin shall not have dominion over you:..." according to the Scriptures.

Have you now seen why you must deal with all self-righteousness? You must deal with selfishness. People go to church and occupy spaces with books, Bibles and even stones. There is no discipline in the church because of selfishness. There is boasting because of self- stubbornness, which is as a result of the self that has refused to submit to the Holy Spirit.

Flesh is responsible for procrastination, laziness, covetousness, and such like. If you don't pull down the shrine of self, the Lord will disqualify you from His army. Disqualification will be the best option because if not, you will become a casualty in the battle field.

There was an old white man in the early 1980s who preached a message title: " How to be miserable." He said the one way to be miserable is to be pre- occupied with or think about oneself. He went on to say that if a man wants to be miserable, he should be talking about himself alone. Everything is about "I" in the life of a miserable man. "I did this. I did that. I, I and I." That's the way to become miserable. This preacher did not stop there. He said to be miserable, a man should mirror himself in the opinion of others. When a life thrives on people's opinions, the individual is on his way to being miserable.

There are many other things the man highlighted that can make a man miserable. Some of them are being suspicious, listening greedily to what people say, expecting to be appreciated for everything one does, becoming jealous and envious, being sensitive to even a little insult, not forgiving offenders and loving yourself supremely above all others. These will make any man or woman miserable. He however said that the greatest factor to become miserable is to allow self to reign in one's life.

You need to pray some serious prayers as you read this book. If you feed the flesh, it will get stronger. The hardest prayer of your life must be targeted towards dethroning self. Conversely, if you feed your spirit, it will get stronger. Jesus said: "The flesh profiteth nothing." You cannot afford to under- estimate the power of the flesh because it will ruin you before you realise it.

Lay your hands on your chest and pray this prayer point.

Every power of the flesh in my life, die, in the name of Jesus.

The shrine of self is the power of sin which functions against the law of God. It makes it impossible to align your life with the law of God.

The shrine of self forbids from spiritual good. The man ruled by it does not profit in any spiritual good.

The shrine of self is what the Bible says cannot please God. It engages in self- satisfaction within.

The shrine of self is the tool the devil uses to control a person's life. This shrine provides legal grounds for satanic activities in a believer's life.

The empty well of life we received from our ancestors is the shrine of self. It is the producer of evil works within. This is the reason repentance is like destroying its works. Repentance only takes care of the works of the flesh. The producer of these works is still within. This must also be dealt with.

The shrine of self is the one responsible for anger.

The shrine of self generates impure thoughts. It is so terrible that it can hold only one area of your life captive. You may be free from one sin yet hooked to another.

The shrine of self can specialise in manifesting one particular sin in a person's life. It is like what doctors do. They study general medicine but specialise in a particular field. There are therefore gynecologists, cardiologists, physiotherapists, anatomists, surgeons, etc. It is not an excuse that you don't fight, commit fornication, etc, but you are controlled by the flesh in one area of your life. Flesh should not be allowed to reign in your life at all.

There is no difference between a witch and a fornicator. They are both apprentices in the training school of the flesh. What the devil does is division of labour. He engages some people in some sins and engages others in some other sins. The bottom line is that the devil is the employer of all such employees in the work of the flesh. No class of satan's employees will inherit the kingdom of God. They will all celebrate their reward in hell fire, except they repent.

The anger that brews in you once in a while is not different from the witchcraft, immorality, etc. of another. Except you repent and allow God to dethrone the flesh in your life, you will end up in hell fire. All works of the flesh will earn the workers thereby the wages of sin, which is death. If you have a mango tree in your compound that you don't want to continue to produce fruit, it is not enough to cut it down, or prune the branches, you need to dig up the roots and destroy them.

If you prune the branches and render the trunk bare, it does not change its capacity for producing fruits. In a conducive condition, it will sprout again and produce fruits as usual. The reason some people have not been found manifesting the work of the flesh is because there is no conducive environment yet.

A sister was disciplined in a church for becoming pregnant before her wedding. When I met her, she surprised me in a great way by her confession. She said she only wanted to be sure that her fiancee was not impotent. The flesh can be quiet for a week or more as though no more there. But when it manifests, you will be very surprised. This is why some pastors can beat up their wives.

The reason some people have not committed fornication is because they are yet to find a partner in the deal. The reason some people are not apprehended yet by members of the police is because they are yet to work in a place they will have access to a lot of money. The day they have such opportunity, flesh will have his way and their seeming innocence will give way.

The solution to the problem of the flesh is to drag it to the cross and nail it there.

The cross, too, does not spare anybody kept under its power. When Jesus was nailed to it, He remained there. The cross kept back the robbers nailed to it. Drag your flesh and self there, nail it once and for all and become free from the powers of the flesh. If you are still reacting uncomfortably as a lady because you are chided or corrected over your indecent dressing, the flesh is still in charge of your life. Your head is tightly covered not because of religious devotion but to hide the worldly attachments fixed on your hair. It is the work of the flesh. You need to pray surgical prayers.

One of the messages I heard that shook my life was a sermon preached in 1976. The sermon was titled: "The battle I will not like to win." "I will like to win battles against witches and wizards, sicknesses and diseases and poverty. But the battle against the Holy Spirit, I don't want to win," the preacher said. He said he desired that the Holy Spirit should defeat him in all areas of his life. What a sermon! That's what we need in this generation. The time is coming that you will pray the last prayer of your life, sing the last song, sleep the last sleep and laugh the last laughter. At that time, the words of the preacher in Ecclesiastes that says: "Vanity of vanities, all is vanity" will become real and clear to you. In the real sense of it, there are no dead people. People are either living on earth, in heaven or hell.

You must decide that the shrine of self must be destroyed in your life. You must pray like Zechariah that "That which dieth (in this case now, the flesh) let it die." You must pray that God should look for a long nail and nail you to the cross. You will no longer be bothered about the things of this world. You will only be waiting to hear "Welcome thou good servant. Enter into the joy of your Lord." The only thing that can hinder you from hearing the welcome address of the Lord of lords is the flesh. You must be more violent in your prayer against it than against the devil and his demons. The moment you have victory over the flesh, satan, demons, the world and sin will lose their powers and influences over you.

The eyes of God are watching you. There was a prophet who wanted to sexually abuse a lady. He mounted so much pressure on her that one day, the lady came to him and as it were, agreed to go to bed with him. This man took her behind his shop, ready to sin. But the lady said that place was too open. He changed venue and took her into his shop, she still said somebody could see them. He kept taking her around until they changed six different rooms. The lady then looked at him and said "You are a disgrace, tell me where God will not see us." That was the disgrace of a prophet who was enjoying the patronage of people coming for his prayers and prophecies. Until your flesh dies, you cannot become what God wants you to become.

What have you that you have not received? Your present position is a privilege from God. Why are you proud of yourself, your position, your achievements as if it's not God that has helped you? You need the surgical knife of God to operate in your life. Pray the prayer points below with all seriousness they deserve.

PRAYER POINTS

1   Power of the cross, crucify my flesh, in the name of Jesus.

2   Every power of the flesh in my destiny, die, in the name of Jesus.

3   Everything in my life that has not manifested now, but will manifest later to destroy my life, die, in the name of Jesus.

4   Any material from my body in the kingdom of darkness, disappear by fire, in the name of Jesus.

5   Every ladder, used by the enemy to climb into my life, be consumed by fire, in the name of Jesus.

CHAPTER 5

WANTED; MEMBERS OF DANIEL BAND

Members of Daniel Band are men and women with purposeful hearts. The first striking quality about prophet Daniel is a purpose of heart. His purpose of heart ignored the threat of a ruling monarch. His purpose of heart made him to close his eyes against the appeal of a royal meal. His purpose of heart made him hold his breath against the aroma of the king's food.

Purpose of heart in the face of many compromises was the first quality in the life of Daniel that God reserves for all time and eternity. You will appreciate Daniel's purpose of heart better if you remember his background.

He was a captive in Babylon. He was given a special privilege of being hosted to the king's meal. From the tables of fellow slaves in Babylon, he was invited to the royalty of the banquet table. For Daniel, so long as what could pass for mere eating and drinking contradicted his religious conviction, he would not bulge.

Members of Daniel's band are desperately needed today. People that will rise against the tide of compromise. God is looking for people that will despise the appeals of worldly pleasure. The heaven of heavens is looking for men and women who will dare to risk their health, souls and life in defence of God's course in the face of most terrible of all dangers.

Daniel had the opportunity to compromise but he did not. God is looking for such people today. He wants to enlist in His army, men and women to whom worldly allurement would amount to nothing. He is looking for people, who would dare to lose their positions, jobs, even their lives in defence of the faith and standard once delivered to the saints.

The righteousness and purpose of Daniel's heart did not immune him from conspiracy and dangers. But these positioned him where he could freely enjoy the support of heaven. The highest council in the Babylon kingdom conspired against him. The conspiracy against him left his life with two options. He was either to compromise his faith, or die cruelly by the claws of hungry lions. He must have been reminded by history that those who were thrown into lions' den did not come out alive. He chose not to compromise and was rounded up. Bound for slaughter, he was to be made a cheap meal for the waiting lions because he would not compromise.

To what extent had your faith been threatened, that you are giving up? Did God forsake Daniel? Not at all! The conspiracy of the world that won the approval of the king only got for Daniel the support of angels commanded by God. "God has sent his angels to keep me from the lions," he tested heroically right in the lions' den after a long night of abode with the wild beasts.

God is looking for members of Daniel's band! As satan is building evil orchestration against you, God is also building super protection around you, so long as you don't compromise.

How many ladies are prostitutes today on account of hunger? How many have sold their pride because of money? How many have shipwrecked their faith because of the promise of promotions?

Daniel was to sit for an exam when his test to stand or compromise came. He stood firm and excelled ten times better than his counterparts.

How did you pass the exam about which you have testified? You gave money as a man and you lavished your body for immorality as a lady? God is looking for members of Daniel's band.

Members of Daniel's band are those who heed God's

command. They are very few indeed. A songwriter said though they are few, honour them who belong to this band.

The call to be part of Daniel's band is a call to stand alone. It is not easy to stand alone. But only those who dare to stand alone have a record to themselves written with the pen of God. Eagles don't fly in a flock. Reaching an altitude beyond the imagination of the majority is not a collective affair. It is your purpose of heart. It is your determination. It is your pursuit.

In the call to stand alone, your spouse may not stand with you. In your response to the fearlessness of confronting evil, your friends may disagree with you. In fact, Daniel had more enemies than friends. They suffer more conspiracies than enjoying men's support.

Did anybody conspire against those that ate the king's meal in the days of Daniel? Did anybody conspire against those that refused to hold the sceptre of prayer steady in Daniel's days? Not at all.

To answer the Daniel call is to dare to stand alone, no matter the consequences.

You look out in the sky and you won't find many eagles in a flock. Those who want to fly high don't flock. They stand alone. Men and women who have changed this world are those going to the opposite direction to the majority.

John Wesley threw his brilliant academic career into

the gospel work and England considered it a waste in those days. He pioneered the holiness movement with over forty thousand sermons to his record. He became the founder and father of the Methodists who terribly shook their generation.

Members of Daniel Band are those who have re-written the history of the world. They changed kingdoms. They replaced iniquitous culture and norms with principles of righteousness.

Martin Luther swam against the tides in his own time. He laid his brilliance at the foot of the cross and canvassed the crusade of "The just shall live by faith" against the monument of Catholicism in his age.

Men and women who changed the world were unconventional. They were strange. They responded to the order from above against the orders of this world.

Will you become a member of Daniel's band?

It is not easy to be a lone ranger. Dare to have a purpose of heart? Let the world know what you stand for. When people know what you stand for, they know what to bring to you.

Another songwriter said: "Many mighty men are lost who could not stand. They could have been great for God if they had joined the Daniel's band." He went on to say: "Many giants, strong, great and tall who are boasting through the land would fall headlong to hell, if Daniel's band confronted them."

The giants boasting about in our time do so because they are yet to be confronted by members of Daniel's band.

When I look at a congregation of believers, I wonder how many people are willing to become members of Daniel's band. Many people come to MFM but are not real members. They are yet to connect with the spirit of MFM. Attendance does not make you a member. Some people only come to a place of worship like this to quench the fires of the enemies. God is not looking for such people. He is looking for battle axes and weapons of war. He is looking for members of Daniel's band. God is not interested in those who don't take their salvation serious.

Unfortunately for some people that worship here with us, they don't even understand the ministry and mission of MFM, yet they assume to be members. Some people who are not members brand us a strange church. They are very, very correct. We are not like other churches. You were not there when the Lord gave me the covenant for the ministry. You don't know what He told me. I have a copy of that blue print from Him but you don't. If you therefore do as you are bidded in this church, you will know miracles have not started yet because of what shall begin to happen. Until you begin to follow the blue print from the Lord, you are yet to really know what MFM is all about.

Many years ago I took some questions to the Lord. I

said, "Lord but there are people here committing adultery, telling lies, sisters still dress like Jezebel on the streets, witches and wizards are still here. And He said to me that I should not bother myself about them that they are wasting their time. He said they are not members of MFM. The Lord said they only come here to chorus loud hallelujah when you say "praise the Lord."

You must decide whether you want to belong or not. You must decide whether you want to do God's will or not.

Many times I have seen ladies dress in an indecent manner. Their dresses are so revealing that one couldn't imagine them ever going to a living church. Some of them wear tight fitting dresses that reveal all their physique, yet they are associated with living churches, even MFM. I wonder how some ladies wear those things because it would appear that they need assistance to pull the dresses off them. If those ladies coming to our church would follow the total teachings of this place, they would experience and enjoy more of God's miracles than before.

How can somebody who attends a living church put on what they call *spaghetti*? You do that to expose your privacies. As a man, what need, is there for you, coming to a gospel church wearing chains? Are you a slave? If your concept about church is a house of fashion, you are committing an error worthy of taking you to hell.

If you want to be a member of Daniel's band, you will

dare to stand alone. You will dare to have a purpose of heart. You will dare to make the purpose known.

When you are on the Mountain of fire, you receive fire and miracles begin to manifest. That is the true spirit of MFM. You climb the mountain, receive the fire and manifest the miracles.

My phone rings many times from people, who although are members of other churches, need prayers because of their peculiar problems. Whenever I ask them why they choose to call me despite having General Overseers in their own churches, they tell me that their G. O. don't understand. Even some members of MFM nowadays boast in their G. O. and encourage others to come and see me. They do not understand that it is not the intention of God to keep fire in only one man or one place.

You are supposed to have so much fire and power that before you recommend anybody to come and see me, you should have given the person a spiritual first aid. What are you doing that you are bereft of power and fire? You are supposed to handle personally the cases of those you are sending to me, as a member of MFM.

This ministry operates on the principle of "operation do-it-yourself." We don't make anybody slave to pastors, prophets or anybody in this place. If you want to be a member of Daniel's band, you need to understand what I am talking about. MFM is a movement. You can see it affecting other churches around.

There are different services and operations in an army. Some soldiers are drivers, some are dentists, some nurses, some only operate on ceremonial days, like Independence Day and such like. Some perform some menial tasks for their superior's wives, etc. But when there is war, some special soldiers are dispatched to go to battle fronts. They are called combatant soldiers. This group is where MFM belongs. We can't be compared to others.

A woman ignorantly picked up a grenade he found by the road on her way to the market, during the Nigerian civil war. She just put it in her basket of yams because she was a civilian who didn't know what she picked. She thought of taking it home as a toy for her children. Unfortunately for her, a tuber in the basket detonated the grenade and her basket of yams went a different direction while her head went another. A soldier wouldn't do that because he knows the implication of toying with a grenade.

You now understand why we scream about certain things here and some people wonder why. Those people wondering why are spiritual politicians, they are not soldiers.

Some were given two holes in the ear lobes by their mothers. They went further to add extra without knowing the implications. A soldier recognizes the weapons of the enemies as soon as he sees them. Others seem to tell God that their hair is too short, therefore justifying fixing attachments on the hair. When we raise an alarm here, they don't understand. They feel we are trying to add something to the gospel. They wonder why we scream when we discern danger.

I read a story in the dailies recently. A lady went to a saloon to braid her hair. This event took place in Calabar. She was billed double of what she should pay because her dresser promised her to work very fast. She was warned that she should not look at the mirror while they fixed her hair. She agreed. Somehow, she forgot the warning and brought out her own mirror from her hand bag and looked at it. To her surprise, she found more than six hands working on her hair and screamed. The saloonist ran out and has not been reported found up till now. Where do you go with hair fixed by two visible and four invisible hands?

Look at the Bible verse below to discover the first characteristic of the members of Daniel's band.

Psalm 8:9: O LORD our Lord, how excellent [is] thy name in all the earth!

God is an excellent God. His name is excellent in all the earth. The first human being in the Bible who was described as having an excellent spirit was Daniel. Read this account in Daniel five, verse twelve.

Dan.5:12: Forasmuch as an excellent spirit, and knowledge, and understanding, interpreting of dreams, and shewing of hard sentences, and dissolving of doubts, were found in the same Daniel, whom the king named Belteshazzar: now let Daniel be called, and he will shew the interpretation.

If you want to be a member of this band, the first thing you need to pray into your life is the spirit of excellence. This attribute of Daniel is repeated again in the chapter following. Look at the next verse below.

Dan. 6:3: Then this Daniel was preferred above the presidents and princes, because an excellent spirit [was] in him; and the king thought to set him over the whole realm.

If you look at what God put together in these verses that constitute excellence, you will find:

✓   knowledge

✓   understanding

✓   interpretation of dreams

✓   dissolving of hard sentence

✓   dissolving of doubt

These were put together to account for the excellence of Daniel's spirit.

Not everybody will be born a prophet. Not everybody will be born a great person. In fact such people are always very few. The beautiful thing about Daniel's attributes is that you can pray them into your life. God didn't introduce Daniel as a prophet, though he was, but he revealed the attributes that made him outstanding for Isaiah, Jeremiah, Elijah, Elisha, etc. you will find out that God paid particular attention to the fact that they were prophets. Daniel was not given such introduction.

Daniel prayed himself into position, relevance and prominence. What lesson do you learn? You too can pray yourself into relevance. You can pray to change your identity. You can pray to have a name among the heroes of faith.

The more you pray the more you discover. The more you discover, the more direction you have. The more direction you have, the more success you have. The more success you have, the better your destiny becomes.

The first man in the Bible with a qualification of an excellent spirit is Daniel. He was the person God used for the salvation of the magicians. The king had decided to kill all of them for their failure to supernaturally know and interpret a dream. Daniel went to God and got the solution. He was the same person lions could not eat. He was bold and fearless. His life was yielded to God.

Any life yielded to God is simultaneously dedicated to quality. Only the best is good enough for your life. The word of God is that "Let your life so shine so that God may be gloried thereby." The Lord is calling you to pray the spirit of excellence into your life, so that you can belong to Daniel's band.

You can be a spiritually knowledgeable person. Knowledge is both the enemy and opposite of ignorance. The only thing that can kill ignorance is knowledge. It is the only thing that can damage ignorance.

There was a rich man here in Lagos who had a dream. He saw himself in a church where funeral was conducted for somebody. He saw himself in the dream as funeral songs were rendered.   He was part of the entire ceremony. As the funeral songs went on and he sang along something prodded him to find out whose funeral it was. He turned the back of his copy of the programme booklet and found his own photograph there. He started screaming that he wasn't dead and that the song should cease. They told him it was too late that he was already part of the ceremony.

What happened next was frightening. Before that week ran out, his wife and six children were involved in a fatal accident and they all died. The man became unconscious at the sad news. He was fainting. People around tried to revive him. When it was clear that he needed medical attention, he was rushed to the hospital.

On the way to the hospital, the vehicle conveying him had an accident and he, too, died instantly. In just a week, the whole family was wiped out because of ignorance. Somebody with, at least, little knowledge of the Bible would have prayed to scatter the evil congregation, consumed the programme booklet by fire and invoked the power of the Scriptures that says: "I shall not die but live, to declare the works of God."

Short and simple the process appears, but that would have redeemed that family from the power of wasters. Knowledge is power. You must be a man or a woman of knowledge to be a member of Daniel's band. Knowledge will move you forward. It will do great things in your life.

The Lord is calling for people with the spirit of

excellence to belong to Daniel's band. Don't worry about those looking at you. Your look may be dull and not exciting, it doesn't matter. You will soon discover that those in the dark don't have the right to tell you, a child of light, how to run your life. When they run into troubles, they will come back to you.

Knowledge is an essential part of the spirit of excellence. Knowledge is the first benefit of a great thing the Lord starts doing in a man's life.

The second is understanding: Don't be shallow in your understanding of the things of God. Pray to receive the understanding of the word of God so that you can behold the deep and wondrous things in it.

The third thing about the spirit of excellence is interpretation of dreams. Your dream is a spiritual monitor, telling you what's going in your life in the spiritual realm. Dreams are very common experiences. You dream and others do. The best thing is to have the ability to correctly interpret dreams for yourself and for others.

The fourth element of the spirit of excellence is ability to decode hard sentences and five, dissolving doubts in the minds of men.

These five elements make up the spirit of excellence. The Lord is calling for excellence, which interprets the best, the finest of its kind, a first class among classes, the highest quality, extremely good, outstanding and extra-ordinary. These are what excellence means.

Belonging to Daniel's band is a call. I wish the Lord would fill all with the spirit of excellence! I wish the Lord would empower you with the spirit of excellence! Then you will understand the full implication of your call.

Wanted, members of Daniel's band!

Dare to be a Daniel. Dare to stand alone.

Daniel stood alone in his time. He led a strange life. His prayer life was strange. His manner of talking was strange. Everything about him was strange. He never joined the crowd. He was a solitary life. When prayer was forbidden by a royal decree, he damned the consequences and prayed. When he was thrown into the lions' den, the Lord delivered and preserved him. When his conspirators were thrown into the same den to replace him, they were devoured to bones by the beasts.

The world is going in a direction, we should go in God's direction. You need not copy the world because light does not copy darkness.

There are pastors' wives who are worldly. They paint their nails, lips, faces and fix their hair in worldly manners. I do not stand to judge them because I don't know what department they are in the army of God. Maybe they belong to advertisement departments. But in our church here, those enjoying the breakthroughs of God are pastors who believe in holiness within and without. There is no need to bother about those who don't. Time will tell.

In the 1970s, we told some people the truth about deliverance and holy living. They despised it and opted for new generation churches where they were made to believe that they could claim anything from God and have it. They knew the Bible but did not know God. As time went on, one after the other they began to realise that the idolatry of their fathers had implications on their lives. Nobody told them what to do next as they began to re-appraise the truth they have been told for so long. Some of them are old now. They are screaming in prayers today. Don't wait for the enemies to mock you. Don't wait for the enemies to mess up your life.

I was invited by a sister to her mother's burial in 1994. This woman was a core immoral woman. She had seven marriage certificates. It was difficult to identify her husband. The lady decorated the corpse with lips stick and fixed its hair as well. It was painted all over with artificial nails fixed on its fingers and toes. Those were days of more spiritual radicalism, so I told the sister that the woman was going to hell, asking her the need for such paintings and decorations. The sister said it wasn't true that with that appearance at the gate of heaven, she would be invited in at once.

The time is coming that everything about your life would come to an end. The money you are crazy about will be put in your hand and you won't be able to hold it. At death, those you were trying to impress with artificial beauty will despise your putrefying corpse. Those you are trying to satisfy now will be the first to say that wicked man or woman is gone. At your burial, a pastor would say "The Lord giveth, the Lord taketh away. Blessed be the name of the Lord." They wouldn't know that "the Lord giveth" indeed but carnality and worldliness have taken away to satan's credit.

Remember, you will close your eyes one day and can't continue with the work taking all your time and attention now. When you die, somebody else will take over the job. The children you leave behind may even fight each other over your legacy after you have died. This is the time you have to re-adjust your life. This is the time you have to re-adjust your destiny. This is the time you have to decide to join the Daniel's band. You won't mind whatever names you are called. So long as you know what you are doing and where you are going, it doesn't matter what people say about or against you. You should only be concerned with your goal and be motivated by the reward of your calling.

Having read about Daniel's band, what is your decision? Having been told that God is looking for members to join the band, what is your decision? Having realised that death is inevitable, how do you want to live the rest part of your life? Decide now. Tomorrow may be too late for you in particular.

Go to the Lord in prayers. Tell Him to forgive you in all areas you have co-operated with the enemies in your life. Get enlisted in Daniel's band. Tell Him you want to be the kind of person He wants you to be. Pray. Tell the Lord to remove from your life anything that can hinder you from being a member of Daniel's band. Tell the Lord you want to be filled with knowledge, understanding, ability to interpret dreams, and hard sentences and the power to be dissolving doubts. These will translate and transform you into a man, a woman of excellent spirit.

Part of the blue print of God for this church is that we should not be involved in any form of artificiality. The safest thing to do is to remain as clean, pure and natural as God made you. Any attempt to modify the image of God is artificiality. Anything you put on or wear that does not glorify God will put you in trouble. The church of God is not a fashion parade centre. It is where the power of God is brought down. The reason we have MFM and you are a beneficiary of God's miracles through the ministry is because we are following the blue print.

God told Moses, "Take heed that you may do everything according to the pattern shown you on the mount." There is a pattern for us. If Moses didn't follow the pattern, miracles would not happen. I therefore dare to tell those dressing indecently and worldly-like to our church that they are not helping the full and further manifestation of the power of God.

Make up your mind where you intend to belong. Will you be a member of Daniel's band? The decision is yours.

PRAYER POINTS

1 Every conspiracy against my destiny in the heavenlies, scatter by fire, in the name of Jesus.

2 Every conspiracy against my progress in the heavenlies, scatter by fire, in the name of Jesus.

3 Every power issuing death curses against me, appear, in the name of Jesus.

4 Every power troubling my destiny from my sleep, die, in the name of Jesus.

5 Every curse of sorrow targeted against me, backfire, in the name of Jesus.

Other Publications by Dr. D. K. Olukoya

1. Be Prepared
2. Breakthrough Prayers For Business Professionals
3. Brokenness
4. Criminals In The House of God
5. Dealing With Local Satanic Technology
6. Dealing With Witchcraft Barbers
7. Dealing With Hidden Curses
8. Dealing With The Evil Powers of Your Father's House
9. Dealing With Unprofitable Roots
10. Deliverance: God's Medicine Bottle
11. Deliverance By Fire
12. Deliverance From Spirit Husband And Spirit Wife
13. Deliverance of The Conscience
14. Deliverance of The Head
15. Drawers of Power From The Heavenlies
16. Dominion Prosperity
17. Evil Appetite
18. Facing Both Ways
19. Fasting And Prayer
20. Failure In The School Of Prayer
21. For We Wrestle . . .
22. Holy Cry
23. Holy Fever
24. How To Obtain Personal Deliverance (Second Edition)
25. Is This What They Died For?
26. Limiting God
27. Meat For Champions
28. Overpowering Witchcraft
29. Personal Spiritual Check-up
30. Power Against Coffin Spirits

Other Publications by Dr. D. K. Olukoya

31. Power Against Destiny Quenchers
32. Power Against Dream Criminals
33. Power Against Local Wickedness
34. Power Against Marine Spirits
35. Power Against Spiritual Terrorists
36. Power Must Change Hands
37. Pray Your Way To Breakthroughs (Third Edition)
38. Prayer Rain
39. Prayer Strategies For Spinsters And Bachelors
40. Prayer Warfare Against 70 Mad Spirits
41. Prayers To Destroy Diseases And Infirmities
42. Praying To Dismantle Witchcraft
43. Release From Destructive Covenants
44. Revoking Evil Decrees
45. Satanic Diversion Of The Black Race
46. Silencing The Birds of Darkness
47. Smite The Enemy And He Will Flee
48. Spiritual Warfare And The Home
49. Strategic Praying
50. Strategy Of Warfare Praying
51. Students In The School Of Fear
52. The Enemy Has Done This
53. The Evil Cry of Your Family Idol
54. The Fire Of Revival
55. The Great Deliverance
56. The Internal Stumbling Block
57. The Lord Is A Man Of War
58. The Prayer Eagle
59. The Pursuit of Success
60. The Secrets of Greatness

Other Publications by Dr. D. K. Olukoya

61. The Serpentine Enemies
62. The Slow Learners
63. The Snake in The Power House
64. The Spirit Of The Crab
65. The Tongue Trap
66. The Way of Divine Encounter
67. The Vagabond Spirit
68. Unprofitable Foundations
69. Victory Over Satanic Dreams (Second Edition)
70. Violent Prayers Against Stubborn Situations
71. War At The Edge of Breakthroughs
72. When God Is Silent
73. Wealth Must Change Hands
74. When You Are Knocked Down
75. Woman! Thou Art Loosed.
76. Your Battle and Your Strategy
77. Your Foundation and Destiny
78. Your Mouth and Your Deliverance
79. Adura Agbayori (Yoruba Version of the Second Edition of Pray Your Way to Breakthroughs)
80. Awon Adura Ti Nsi Oke Nidi (Yoruba Prayer Book)
81. Pluie de Prières
82. Esprit Vagabondage
83. En Finir avec les Forces Maléfiques de la maison de Ton Père
84. Que l'envoûtement perisse
85. Frappez l'adversaire et il fuira
86. Comment recevoir la délivrance du Mari et de la Femme de Nuit
87. Comment se delvrer soi-même
88. Pouvoir Contre les Terroristes Spirituels
89. Prières de Percées pour les hommes d'affaires

90. Prier Jusqu'à Remporter la Victoire

91. Prières Violentes pour humilier les problèmes opiniâtres

92. Le Combat Spirituel et le Foyer

93. Bilan Spirituel Personnel

94. Victoire sur les Rêves Sataniques

95. Prayers That Bring Miracles

96. Let God Answer By Fire

97. Prayers To Mount With Wings As Eagles

98. Prayers That Bring Explosive Increase

99. Prayers For Open Heavens

100. Prayers To Make You Fulfill Your Divine Destiny

101. Prayers That Make God To Answer and Fight By Fire

102. Prayers That Bring Unchallengeable Victory and Breakthrough Rainfall Bombardments

ALL OBTAINABLE AT:

☞ 322, Herbert Macaulay Street, Sabo, Yaba, P. O. Box 12272, Ikeja, Lagos.

☞ IPFY Music Konnections Limited, 48, Opebi Road, Salvation Bus Stop (234-1-4719471, 234-8033056093)

☞ All MFM Church branches nationwide and Christian bookstores.